Sometimes I'm In My Feelings 2

Anna Black

Cole Hart Presents
www.colehartsignature.com

Published by Cole Hart Presents

ISBN 13: 978-1546587705
ISBN 10: 1-54658-770-5

First Trade Paperback Printing May 2017
Printed in the United States of America

10 9 8 7 6 5 4 3 2 1

Dedication

This book is dedicated to my readers, whom I truly appreciate and I hope that I can make my readers laugh, cry and reflect. I am so excited to release book number two and I hope you guys want to read book three. I am so happy to be able to entertain with words and I am excited that you decided to read ***Sometimes I'm In My Feelings*** 2. This goes to you, my readers; you are the reason to do what I do.

Enjoy!

Acknowledgments

Always thanks to the Most High for his many, many blessings. I would name names, but I'd hate to forget to mention anyone, so thanks to my readers, family and friends that have encouraged me, supported me and been there for me when I needed you. Thanks to my publisher, editor, cover designer and all that helped me to produce this novel. Hugs and kisses to my guy Gregory, my daughter Tyra and my doggies Jaxson and Jasmine. My two moms, Lue and Charlotte and my daddy Marvin Sr., who is no longer with me, thanks for doing your best to raise me to be the woman I am today. And I have to give a shout out to my two bestie's that has purchased, read and supported me since I wrote my very first sentence for a novel, Chanda and Dominique. You two have given me more than support, you've motivated me to push forward, no matter what hurdles came my way, love you!

I am grateful to God for so many blessings. To have a creative mind is a gift and I thank Him. To allow my stories to be enjoyed by others is also a blessing. Thank you, my readers, for giving **Sometimes I'm In My Feelings 2** a chance to be read by you.

Also by Anna Black

Now You Wanna Come Back *Series*
Who Do I Run To?
Who Do I Run To Now?
Split Image
I'm Doin' Me *Series*
The Side Effects of You

Short Stories

If I Wasn't for Tony
Mr. Wrong
I Just Wanna Be Loved
Hooks In Me
My First and Last Love

Anthologies

Cougar Cocktales
Full Figured 10

Coming Soon

Thug Passion Marks Series
Lovin' the Chase
Foolish

"Feelings Deep Enough To Swim In"

"Be You, Do You, & Love You"

Chapter One

Legacy

Legacy balled her fists at her sides as she glared at the woman in her living room claiming she was pregnant with Kenny's child. Legacy debated if she should charge her and take her ass down, or handle things like a civilized adult and take Tanya's word at face value. Her instincts wanted to tackle her to the floor, but she decided on the latter and asked, "How do you know this baby is Kenny's?"

"Are you serious, Legacy? Kenny and I not too long ago broke up. We were living together, and we shared the same got'damn bed!" she barked.

"A bed that has been cold for weeks," Kenny interjected.

Tanya turned to him. "I'm twelve weeks along, Kenny, so there it is. At that time, our bed was pretty damn hot as I recall," she snapped back, placing a hand on her right hip.

"This is crazy. When did you figure this out, LaTanya? I've only been gone for all of three weeks, and you're telling me you didn't know before now?" he questioned.

"Yes, Tanya, when did you find out you were pregnant?" Legacy inquired.

"I knew for a little while. I mean, I had a feeling, but I got confirmation today."

"I don't believe your ass, and this bullshit is fucking comical," Kenny said. He took a seat on the arm of the chair next to where he had been posted since the alleged pregnant one walked into the door.

"I knew you'd act this way!" Tanya cried. She sniffled and then went into her purse and pulled out a piece of paper and stretched out her arm towards him. After a brief pause, he took it. "Here … I had an ultrasound done, and this is no lie, Kenny, or a joke. I am pregnant, and it is yours. We are having a baby."

"So, that's your decision, Ms. Thang, just to keep it? Shouldn't Kenny have a say in this?" Legacy chimed in.

"He can say whatever the fuck he wants to say, but there are no other options. I'm having my baby," Tanya shot at her. Legacy could see the seriousness in her eyes. Her tone was firm, so she was sure the bitch was going through with her pregnancy.

"Hold on, hold on. Just hold on, aw'ight? If in fact this is my baby, we are keeping it," Kenny established.

Legacy shot him a look. "Ex-fucking-cuse me!" Legacy bellowed and put a hand on her hip and twisted her neck.

"Lay, calm down. You know me, and an abortion is not an option for my kid. If there is any possibility that I'm the father, I will be a father, Legacy. Tanya and I were in a relationship. We had sex like people do in relationships, and even though Ms. LaTanya here was supposed to have been on birth control, I have to take responsibility for my kid, just like I have for our two."

"I was, Kenny," Tanya insisted.

"Hummm, I bet," Legacy mumbled.

"Legacy, honestly, this is none of your got'damn business. This is between Kenny and me," she barked at her.

"Oh no, bitch, you can bring that shit down. You ain't gon' come up in my house yelling and taking command. Anything that goes on with this man from now on is my business, and if this little bundle you're carrying is his, you will have to deal with me and him for a very long time."

"Bitch, I don't have to deal with shit!" she shot back but Kenny interrupted.

"Enough!" he yelled over them. "Enough you two. This ain't about you, Legacy, and this certainly ain't about you, LaTanya. This is about the baby you claim I fathered. There is no secret that Legacy and I are back together and plan to get married, so this here will be a family thing and for the sake of my children, there will be no bitches, name calling, disrespect or back and forth with you two. Got it!" he declared.

Both Legacy and Tanya stood in silence. Legacy wasn't afraid of Kenny, and she'd normally have a word or two for his ass, but he was right. She demanded respect as his kids' mother, so if Tanya was truly the mother of his child, she'd cool her heels and let them decide what the best solution was for them. She had to put all her personal feelings about that bitch to the side and be a part of a solution to this fucked up situation.

No matter how good things are going, something fucked up always brings you back to the harsh fucking reality that we live in an imperfect world. "Okay, Kenny. You're right. I will try to keep my personal feelings for her in check, but Tanya needs to know how to stay in her fucking lane," Legacy added. She planned to give that bitch just as much respect as Tanya gave her.

"Legacy, you always got something to fucking say, that's why I can't stand yo' fat ass," Tanya shot back.

Legacy glared at Kenny with a, *you betta get yo' bitch look.* She was five seconds away from beating a pregnant bitch to the white meat.

"LaTanya, that's enough. You need to leave now!" Kenny told her and pointed at the door. She didn't budge. He stood and opened the door, and she looked at him like he was crazy.

"You just gon' throw me out?" she cried in disbelief.

"Fuck yeah! If you think you gon' stand in my house and disrespect Legacy, you got shit twisted. I'll come by tomorrow so we can finish this conversation."

"No, *we'll* be by tomorrow to finish this conversation," Legacy corrected. Tanya stood there for a moment before heading to the door.

"Bye, Kenny," she sighed and made her exit. As soon as she cleared the doorway, Kenny shut the door.

He looked at Legacy, and her eyes grew large with tears. "Awww, baby. I'm so sorry," Kenny apologized and quickly moved to hold her.

"Could it really be yours, Kenny? You were fucking her raw?" He was quiet. "I knew you were fucking her, that I knew, but I had no idea you were over there making fucking babies."

"Shhhh, come on, baby. I wasn't over there trying to make no damn babies with Tanya. She was supposed to be on the got'damn pill. I used condoms, but not every single time. I'm so sorry. This is the last thing I wanted. You gotta know that."

She sniffled. "I know that, Kenny, and I believe you, but fuck. This was supposed to be our happy ending. Me, you and our girls and maybe a son one day. This is not what I envisioned for us."

"Neither did I, but it is what it is. You know damn well I wasn't trying to father no kids with anyone other than you. If this baby is mine, I have to do the right thing and be a father to that baby whether I like it or not."

"I know, but it fucking hurts!" she sobbed. He held her tight. She was outdone, and he knew how upset she was because he let her cry as long as she needed. Finally, they climbed into bed. She was in no mood to make love, but Kenny begged to feel her insides. He said he wanted to feel as close as he could to her, and making love would confirm their connection. She didn't deny him and was happy that she opened wide for him because his loving reaffirmed their closeness, and she fell asleep easily after in his arms.

Chapter Two

Anika

When she opened her eyes to the smell of bacon in the air, she smiled brightly. She had been at Jaxson's for the past couple of nights avoiding her loft and Rey's back-to-back calls and text messages. Jaxson was the sweetest, and he had been doing everything in his power to keep her smiling and not crying over Reynard's trifling gay ass. She had a few moments when she broke down and cried, but Jaxson was right there to kiss her tears away.

She sat up and let her legs dangle on the side of his king-sized bed. She stretched and let out a long yawn. She had slept well, more like a damn baby in Jaxson's strong arms, and she couldn't wait to head downstairs just to kiss his lips. She hurried to the bathroom to release all the wine that filled her bladder from the evening before. It was her turn to cook last night, and she had made the most amazing chicken stuffed poblano peppers she had ever made in her days of cooking. That was a dish she had mastered, but she spiced it up by changing the cheese from mozzarella to Monterey Jack and added mushrooms and Spanish rice into them.

Jaxson was blown away and gave her praises for such an excellent dish, and they easily drank two bottles of white wine. With heavy flirting, kissing and touching, they had played a long game of pool. After Jaxson literally beat her panties off, she was spread wide open on his pool table as he introduced his tongue to her clit. They'd had sex before, but that was the first oral experience she'd had with Jaxson. He was gentle, sweet and took his time, and just when she thought he'd spare her body, he turned into a beast. He sucked, probed, licked and bit her in places she never imagined.

By the time he pushed his rock hard dick inside of her soaked pussy, she was already exhausted from the other two orgasms he had given her. When he caressed her legs with his fingertips while he stroked her soft center, her moans grew louder, and when he kissed the soles of her feet, her head spun. She felt his hot mouth wrap around her big toe and when he sucked on it, her body shook. Waves shot up to her pleasure box, and she came hard and felt her own love nest contract. She had never been turned on so much or felt so sexy before that session with Jaxson. He paid attention to every inch of her body, and kissing her feet and sucking her toes took her to a level she thought she'd never reach.

After she brushed her teeth, washed her face and did a quick brush of press power and lip gloss, she put on his Bulls jersey and headed down to the kitchen.

"Good morning," she spoke before taking a seat at the island.

"Good morning, beautiful," Jaxson smiled.

"Why are you dressed already?" she questioned. It was Sunday, and she didn't expect to see him up and ready to leave the house, nor did she expect to see him in work attire.

He smiled. "It's the Patel's. They want to meet for brunch after church and tell me what house they chose. They are now ready to put in an offer."

"Your million-dollar budget couple?" she beamed. "Honey, that is great!"

"Yes, so I have to work on my off day because this sale is important."

"Hey," she said and took a sip of the juice from the glass that Jaxson had placed in front of her. "It's all worth it. I mean, that is a huge deal, babe."

"Yes, so I made you some breakfast, sleepy head. I'm heading out in a minute."

"Thanks, JT. I didn't mean to sleep this late, but somebody in this room wore me out. I am exhausted."

He walked over to her side and turned her to face him. "Well, you need to get all the rest you need while I'm out because when I come home, I want to have you again, Anika. Your body, your love and your … you know, feel so damn good."

"My what, Jaxson? Don't be shy, say the word."

He hesitated and then said, "Your pussy, baby. It's so damn good. If I didn't have to leave, I'd lift your ass up on this island and fuck the shit outta you right here and now."

NeNe's pussy throbbed. "Baby, please just put it in. I was cool until you came up on me smelling so fucking good. Just put it in, you won't be late," she encouraged.

"As soon as I get home, baby, I promise." He backed away. "I must go." He went over to the counter, grabbed her plate and put it in front of her. "Enjoy your breakfast, baby. As soon as I get two signatures and send it over to the seller's agent, I'll be home."

"Okay, baby. I'm so proud of you, JT, and I'm happy for you."

He smiled at her. "Thanks. Now eat your breakfast. I hope you enjoy it, I'll be home soon." He gave her a nice wet kiss, grabbed his briefcase and keys and was out the door.

NeNe glanced down at her plate. The waffle, scrambled eggs and bacon looked like it had been served on a five-star restaurant dish. The fresh fruits in a bowl a few inches from her orange juice looked delectable, so NeNe wasted no time and ate every bit of her breakfast. When she finished, she cleaned the kitchen the way she would clean her own. She opened a few closet doors and soon found the broom, mop and vacuum and got to work. She dusted his shelves and had the house smelling like Pine-sol by the time she finished.

After she headed upstairs to shower and put on something comfortable, a nap was needed, but as soon as she climbed into Jaxson's bed, she got a text from Rey.

I c u r not comin home anytime soon. I knew u were fuckin' that cat..

I'll go home when u r gone Reynard. It doesn't matter who I'm fucking! I would be home only fucking u, but now that ur gay, that shit will never happen, ever again!

I'm not gay, and by the end of the day I'll be outta yo' spot. U don't know shit about me & Lisa!

I know she or should I say he has a dick!

Think what the fuck u wanna think Nene. I loved u, but it is what it is & I've never cheated on u with her!

What the fuck ever Rey! Save that bullshit 4 someone who gives a fuck gay boi!

With that, he didn't reply. NeNe tossed her phone and took her much needed nap. When she woke, Jaxson had not come home yet. She went downstairs and it was after six. Why she slept so long was crazy, but she had been keeping late nights with Jaxson. She turned on the tube and after twenty minutes, she sent him a text.

Bae, where u at?

After another twenty minutes, she gets, ***On my way now. I'm sorry sweetheart.***

No sorry needed. I know duty calls.

True, but I was with my ex Michelle. I'll explain when I get in.

Should I leave?

Baby no…it was nothing. I'll explain as soon as I get home. Please don't leave.

Not sure what came over her, but panic kicked in. What reason would Jaxson have to see his ex? Why would he have to explain anything? She hopped up and ran upstairs to get her purse and keys. Nene wasn't in the mood for anymore bullshit and certainly wasn't up for heartbreak from Jaxson.

She looked around and decided she'd take all her shit now because coming back wasn't an option.

She loaded her Mustang and before she made it home, Jaxson called. She hit ignore and questioned her character. "What the fuck is wrong with you, NeNe? You leave one man and fall into the arms of another without a pause," she scolded. "I don't deserve anymore heartache, and Jaxson, you will not make me another subject of pain," she declared. She parked and was grateful not to see Rey's SUV. She hoped he was gone and that all his shit was out.

Nene went up to her unit, and when she opened to the door to a cold and empty loft, she wrapped her arms around herself. Rey had taken more than his share of items from the place, but she didn't give a shit, she was just glad he was gone. She went straight to the thermostat and turned on the heat because September was approaching and the changes in the weather were already taking place, so she definitely needed to heat up her now man-less space.

She went into her bedroom and saw the mess Rey left and shook her head. "Motherfuckas like you would do this stupid shit," she cringed.

She put her bag down and got busy. She cleaned, straightened and worked effortlessly to get her place back to normal. After two hours of non-stop work, she took a break and poured herself a glass of wine and then checked her phone. She had over ten messages from Jaxson and several missed calls.

"Whatever," she mumbled and put her phone down. "I thought you were—," she started to say, but then there was a banging at her door. She knew it was Rey because he left his key on the counter and only locked the bottom lock. As much as she knew being at Jaxson's wasn't where she needed to be, she wished she was there. She snatched the door open braced for a battle, but it was Jaxson to her surprise.

"What, what, what are you doing here?" she stuttered.

"Why did you leave?" he demanded. His tone was unfamiliar to Anika. She had never heard that sound come out of him.

"Listen, JT, it's clear that—," she tried to answer.

"Nothing is clear," he cut her off, coming in close to her. "I want you, and when I got home to see that you were gone, it did something to me, Anika. I called and texted you. There is nothing going on with me and my ex, and I wish you would have stayed and waited for me to explain. Michelle's mother is ill, dying from cancer, and she asked me to come by to see her. She is in her final moments of life, NeNe. Even though our relationship went to crap, we shared family. If you would have waited at my place like I asked you, I would have told you this."

She stood there speechless at first, but she found her voice. "I can't be played by another man, Jaxson."

"Baby, I know that, and I'm the real deal. I know your heart is fragile. I know your emotions are high, and you are scared, but please don't compare me to him. Don't weigh us on what you had with him. Give me a fair chance and if I fuck up, let it be my fuck up, but never compare me to him. You are perfect for me. When I'm near you, I want to consume you, Anika, and when we are apart, you are the only woman on my mind. I don't know when this happened, but it happened, and I want you. I crave you, I need you," Jaxson confessed. He pushed the door shut with his foot, and it slammed shut.

NeNe stood frozen. She tried to digest his words, but she was terrified. She had trusted Rey's words, but everything Jaxson said sounded beautiful, but what if he and his ex reconnected? NeNe couldn't see past pain, all she saw were trust issues. How could she believe him? Rey once told her that same old bullshit. She held her breath and didn't question or challenge his words out loud. She just let him take her body. He undressed her and licked and sucked every inch of her body. When he pushed his dick inside of her, she gasped because she felt like he had entered her body for the first time. Every stroke made her moan. He kissed, licked and touched her body showing her more love and affection than she had ever experienced in her life. Yes, Rey had good dick, but Jaxson made love to her entire body. His kisses were more intense, and the way he touched her was like a lover who cherished his mate.

When they finally finished their night of passion, she lay on his chest and decided to trust him. He wasn't Rey, and she couldn't make him accountable or responsible for the hell Rey had put her through. "I'm sorry," she whispered.

He rubbed her arm and shoulder. "Why are you apologizing, bae?" Jaxson inquired.

"For not trusting you and leaving. I must get use to taking a man's word again, JT. I'm sorry for treating you like him. I know you're not Rey, and I'll try to trust you."

"Baby, I will be patient with you. I'm not the perfect guy, but I can promise you that I have only good intentions for you, for us, and I'll never hurt you, NeNe."

She didn't respond. She just closed her eyes and drifted off to sleep.

Chapter Three

Mia

"Ahh! Yes, daddy, lick that clit. Yes, baby, do my pussy right," Mia moaned. Morris was licking her sweet spot for the second time that night, and Mia laid there trying to concentrate on Morris while putting Rene's stupid ass out of her mind. Morris was the man of her dreams, but she couldn't stop thinking of Rene's two-timing ass. She'd see him at the office and cream her panties. They would be in a meeting, and her eyes would lock with his. She almost opened her legs for him the day before. She was in her office late, and he tapped on her door frame.

"Yes," she answered. When she looked up and saw his ass, she cringed. "Rene, what in the fuck could you possibly want? Seeing you and your pathetic wife in Vegas the other week was enough. I've kept my distance, so why in the fuck are you standing in my office doorway?"

He walked in without words and shut the door. "Enough with this bullshit, Mia. I've been fucking calling you and texting you, but you've ignored me. I miss the fuck outta you, and I want your pussy so fucking bad."

She laughed loudly. "Rene, turn your ass around and vacate my office. I'm done and over your ass. I am not thinking of your ass anymore because I have someone new."

"You've moved on?" he asked, surprised.

"Fuck yeah! You chose Laurie, remember? I'm sweet and lovable, but I'm not a fucking fool, Rene. Go home to

your damn wife. You made your choice. I believed your lies, your undying love for me and 'Mia, baby, please be patient, I'm going to make you my wife, you will be first'. All bullshit, now get the fuck out of my office!" she yelled.

He stood there staring, not budging. "I know you still love me," he countered.

"That love I still have for you doesn't mean a damn thing, and it's not worth shit. I'm not it. I'm not your fucking choice, and I foolishly waited damn near a year for you. I believed you, Rene, so I'll ask politely, get out of my office," she snapped, but he moved in closer. Mia's eyes danced around the room and she wondered what she could do to keep him far away from her. She wasn't over him, and the last thing she needed was for him to be close to her. "Rene, I'm serious, you need to leave," she mustered up, but he was in her face, and she was pinned against her desk. He grabbed her face and pushed his tongue inside of her mouth. She tried to resist him, but her tongue danced with his. "Please," she begged between kisses. "I don't want you," she tried to say, but eventually he swallowed her words.

When he put his hand up her skirt, her moist opening was a dead giveaway that she wanted him. He lifted her up onto the desk and then played with her core and flicked her bulb, and she allowed his tongue to roll up and down her neck. "Ahhh, Rene, baby, ahhh," she moaned, opening up wider for him. He had undone his belt and pants, and his anaconda was ready to push its way inside, but his cellphone sounded off. "Wifey calling, wifey calling, wifey calling," the ringtone played. "Move, you bastard," Mia growled and shoved him away. "I'm a fucking idiot," she continued. She gave him another shove and hopped off her desk. "You think I'm a whore, a piece of bitch ass meat. Get the fuck out, Rene. Go to your fucking wife and stay the fuck away from me. I'm happy. I have a man who adores me that is stand-up and not fucking married. Stay away from me, Rene. I hate you! Stay the fuck away from me!" she yelled. She pulled her skirt back to its proper position and watched Rene exit her office with a look of defeat, yet determination. She knew at that moment it wouldn't be the last she saw of him.

She sat at her desk and admonished herself for being so damn easy. "Why would you allow him to touch you like that, you damn fool? You are with Morris now. A single, kind and gentle man. His dick is little, but it's good," she tried to convince herself. "But nothing like Rene's, Lord, why am I hooked on that bastard? Please, God, fix me and give me a change of heart. Please, God, let me get over him," she cried and then forced herself to get back to work.

***

She moaned as Morris got her close to her orgasm. Her thighs trembled when she felt the surge of her core contracting. She reached down and grabbed hold of the back of Morris' head and let out a sound of relief and pleasure. Morris had done her right, but not quite like Rene. Rene was just stuck in her heart and mind, and she hated him and herself every time she thought of his ass.

"You ready, baby?" Morris questioned as he put on the condom.

"Yes, baby, push that dick inside of me," she moaned. She wished she could say push that big dick inside of me, but that wasn't the case. She opened wider for him and felt him enter her body. It was small, but still good enough to satisfy her urges, but she still wished it were Rene each and every damn time.

Fuck!

Chapter Four

Rene

As soon as he got into his car, he returned his wife's call. "What is it, Laurie?" he sighed as he loosened his tie. He wished he had chosen his mistress because he dreaded going home. All Laurie did was whine, moan, complain and throw Mia in his face every damn hour on the hour. If his phone rang, she'd frown. "Is that your whore?" she'd spit. If he got a text alert, she was over his shoulders. "That better not be that bitch!" she'd snap, and Rene was sick and tired of her constant mentions of Mia and the third degree she gave him whenever he walked through the door. The only thing that kept her quiet was him fucking her into silence.

Now that she thought Mia had turned him out, she had stepped up her performance, and they now fucked like porn stars. Never did Laurie allow Rene to cum on her tits, face, stomach or ass before, but now she always made him pull out so she could see it. She begged him to cum on her ass if he was hitting from the back, and she'd make him promise that he'd let her suck him off. Rene enjoyed every moment for their lovemaking because she now even let him fuck her in her ass, something that was off limits until that night in Vegas.

After Mia told her that Rene had disclosed so many intimate details, she pleaded for Rene to tell her all the things Mia did to turn him on. He hesitated, but she pressed because she claimed she wanted to be his only desire and the only woman he craved. He then told her all the things he wanted that Mia gave that she didn't.

"That bitch lets you nut in her face, and she swallows your shit?" she asked wide-eyed.

"You said you wanted to know, Laurie, and if what I'm telling you will make things worse—"

"No, no, no, go on. In order for me to move forward, I want to know what you need. I'm the only woman that should be giving you all you need, Rene. I'm your wife, not that trash!"

"Calm down, Laurie, we are talking. It's not about Mia, remember? You asked me what does she give me that you don't, correct." She nodded her head yes. "So either you want to know, or you don't."

"I do," she whispered. "Go on."

"And we do anal," he said.

Laurie paused and then bit down on her bottom lip. She shook her head and rubbed her hands up and down her thighs. "I, I, I don't, I just don't think I can give you that. I mean, I love you and want you and this marriage, and I want you to be happy and only desire me and my body, but Rene, that's just, that's just..." she continued to shake her head.

"Nasty, is that the word you're searching for?"

"Yes! Yes, that is exactly the word I'm thinking of."

"But you've never even tried it, baby. You don't know the pleasure it will give you too," he coaxed, caressing the back of her hands. He pulled her fingers to his lips and kissed them.

"That's what you like? I mean, that is some gay shit."

"How so? I want it with a woman, Laurie. I have no desire to fuck a man in the ass. That's not gay. And if two people, meaning a man and a woman enjoy it, how is that gay?"

Laurie sat for a moment or two in silence. Her head hung low. He lifted her chin and kissed her lips. "If you don't like it, we don't have to do it again." It took little convincing and after a few shots and a lot of lubricant, they gave it a go.

The first time wasn't great, the second time didn't seem any better, but that third time, Laurie had an orgasm that make her dig a hole into Rene's skin, and he knew then she was all in.

That was how blissful the rest of their Las Vegas trip was, but once they returned to Chicago and Rene returned to work, all of Laurie's insecurities returned, and she didn't hold back on letting Rene know just how she felt about him and his affair 'with skinny ass Mia' as Laurie would say.

"Why didn't you answer my call?" she shrieked without a hello as soon as she answered.

"I was in the middle of something when you called, baby," Rene said softly. He wanted to normalize the situation as best he could before he got home because he was in no mood for a fight with her.

"In the middle of what, Rene? Mia's thighs?" she shot him.

He wanted to say, "As a matter of fact I was," but he said, "no, Laurie, baby, and please not another episode today about Mia, okay? I'm not thinking about her ass, but somehow you keep bringing her up every damn minute. How can we move on or get past this Mia situation if you can't let it go? This every other day is getting old."

"Because I know you still have a thing for her boney ass. I'm not stupid, Rene, and if I catch your ass with her again, I'm going to kill that bitch, you got that? If you want your little whore to stay amongst the land of the living, you better stay the fuck away from her," she spat.

"Laurie, is this how it's going to be? Is it? Because if it is, we can end this right now. I can't do this with you. Every five minutes it's Mia this or Mia that, or is that bitch Mia in the background, are you with Mia, and this has to stop. Either you trust me, or you don't."

"Trust you, Rene? Are you throwing that word at me? Are you slinging trust at me when you've been banging that bitch for damn near a year?" she quipped.

Rene just gripped the steering wheel and drove while listening to twenty minutes of Laurie's ranting. By the time he got home, she was still yapping about him and his affair, Mia and how he was no good, and yadda, yadda. When he walked into the kitchen door with the phone held up to his ear and she noticed him, she ended the call.

"You're home," she said and took a deep breath. He held up his hand.

"Yes, and enough, Laurie, enough," he said and went over to her. He pulled her into his arms and planted a long hard kiss on her mouth. That was the only way he could get her to shut the fuck up.

"Where are the kids?" he whispered, tugging at her clothes.

"At the sitter's. I wanted to talk to you before picking them up," she tried to say, but he kissed her again. He pulled at her clothes, and before long he had her bent over the arm of the sofa in their family room, fucking her like a wild animal. He slapped her ass cheeks and pulled her hair so hard her back arched, and her face was almost turned up to the ceiling. He pumped hard and took what was his with pleasure. "Take that dick, baby, take it!" he ordered when she panted.

"You're hurting me," she whimpered, but he knew that was code for fuck me harder.

"I'm hurting you, baby, am I killing this pussy?" he groaned in pleasure.

"Yes, daddy, you're hurting me, ahhh, ahhhhh, you're killing my pussy, daddy," she moaned, and that made his dick stiffen even harder.

"You are going to take this dick, you hear me, you're going to take all this dick," he grunted as he stroked harder and slapped her ass cheek even harder. When he was close to nutting, he pulled out and ordered Laurie on her knees. He stroked his shaft over her face, and she waited with her tongue out ready to take his nut in her mouth. "Ahhh shit! Baby, you look so fucking good right now, I'm going to cum all over your face," he growled and shot his thick juices on her face and tongue. That was what he needed. He was grateful he had Laurie to give him that because his days of getting that from Mia were gone, but he had plans to get her back. Whatever he had to do, he was damn sure determined to get Mia back in his good graces and back in his bed.

Chapter Five

Reynard

"Take is slow, baby," Rey instructed Lisa. He had gotten released from the hospital, and Rey paid close attention to everything the doctor said about making sure he had a successful recovery.

"Rey, baby, relax. If I walk any slower, we won't make it to the porch until sundown," Lisa quipped.

"Still got that smart ass mouth. I wish Dr. Shane had a remedy for that."

"Ha-ha," Lisa kidded back. "I just want you to calm the fuck down. I'm not going to over exert myself."

"If you don't take it easy like the doctor ordered, you will."

"Fine, we can take baby steps. Damn!" Lisa spat. It took them a good four or five minutes to make it inside of Lisa's house and once inside, Lisa snapped. "What the hell?" His head went from left to right as his eyes darted over the entire living room.

"I know it's a mess, baby, but when I broke things off with Anika, she told me to leave. I told you I had a few things to bring to your place until I get another spot," Rey quickly explained.

"Awww, hell. Fuck no, Reynard. I don't mind yo' shit being here, but this here bullshit in my living and dining room is un-fucking-acceptable. You know how I keep my place, and this all up in here needs to make its way to the damn basement and off my main floor!" Lisa spat.

"Okay, baby. I will move it all downstairs. It was rush-rush, and with you being in the hospital and me at work, I had to put my shit somewhere before NeNe threw it on the streets."

"What the fuck ever, Reynard. Help me into my Queen Ann bed, give me the remote and make your queen a martini and make all of this," Lisa said dramatically, waving a hand in the air. "Disa-fucking-pear from my living room," he ordered.

"Okay, baby, whatever you say. I got this." He walked Lisa into the bedroom, helped him undress and got him up into his huge bed. He made sure he had the remote, his cellphone and charger and as ordered, he made his favorite Apple Martini against his better judgment. He didn't think he should consume alcohol with his meds, but what diva Lisa wanted, he granted. He had no other place to go, so he had to be on good behavior and in Lisa's good graces until he could get his own place.

"Here's your drink, beautiful, and I will go make your living and dining room look as if my catastrophe never happened."

"Thanks, Rey, and I'm so happy you are here. For you to drop everything and be by my side at the hospital spoke volumes. For you to finally leave and commit yourself to me is all I've dreamed of. Once my body is healed and I can get back to normal, my only goal is to make you happy. I want to prove to you that I was worth choosing," Lisa murmured and touched the back of Rey's hand.

"You don't have to prove a damn thing, baby. I know you're all in. I should have left from jump, but I was too afraid of what this really was. I mean, I struggled with am I gay, am I bi or what the fuck made me fall for a man."

He squeezed his hand. "Rey, I've never been a man. Yes, I was born with a dick, but ever since I've known me, ever since I've known myself, I've known myself as a girl and then a woman. I know it's tough facing this reality, but this is our reality, no one else's, and since you loved me before I completely transitioned, that means you fell in love with Lisa, the person. Not the man or the woman, but with me. I didn't ask to be this way. I don't know why I'm this way or if God hates me or loves me. All I know is I feel complete now, like if God had given me a vagina and tits from jump, no one would have teased me, harassed me, bullied me or beat the shit outta me for just wanting to be myself.

"Society doesn't have to accept what we are or what the fuck we choose for ourselves, but just respect it. I don't care if they hate what we have as long as they keep their opinions and shit to themselves. Turn your motherfucking head and look the other way bitch if you don't like what you see, and let me be me. It's hard enough trying to make it in this world, but it's always a million times harder when you're different. Trust me, Rey, you are going to face a lot of evil, hating and just plain old ignorant ass people, but as long as we have us, we will make it through."

"How are you so strong?" Rey asked and squeezed his hand tighter.

"I wasn't always this way. I went through so much to be right here today. I lost family, friends, and jobs and got my ass beat to a pulp, but I fought for me, that is why I'm strong now. I only have this one life to live and at the end of the day, I will stand alone with God and however he judges me. All I'll say to him is, you created me this way," Lisa said with a faint smile and glossy eyes.

Rey nodded. He leaned in and kissed his forehead. "You are one of the bravest human beings I've ever met in my entire life."

"Believe it or not, you are too. You are the only one who has stood by me and made me feel like a human and not some freak. I love you, Reynard, and I'm thankful to our God that he allowed me to meet you."

"I'm not a big God man, Lisa, but I'm happy I found someone as unique and fun and as sweet as you."

"I do what I do," Lisa joked.

Rey swatted his covered thigh. "Still conceited."

Lisa sipped his drink. "Even on my worst day hunty, I'm fabulous. Now, go make my main floor look like the one I left before going into surgery."

"Yes, ma'am," Rey said and gave Lisa another quick kiss. He knew it would be awhile before he could penetrate his new body, and he was anxious to see what he'd feel like. He took all but clothes and personal toiletries to the basement. He came back, made Lisa another drink and joined him in bed. They binge watched Spartacus since they both agreed they'd always wanted to watch it. Rey grabbed a beer and made popcorn and undressed before he got into bed.

They talked during the episodes and laughed out loud at their own commentary of the series. Before long, Lisa was sleeping but Rey was still wide awake. He got up and took Lisa's glass and his beer bottles to the kitchen and opened his phone and went to Facebook. The first thing he saw was NeNe's new pictures. She had deleted their relationship status, but didn't delete him as a friend.

He was cool with the selfies he saw, but when he scrolled to see there were a few pictures with Jaxson, he immediately got pissed. "Oh, the fuck!" he said and then stalked her page until he fell asleep.

Chapter Six

Omari

Omari walked into Legacy's building with two, five-gallon buckets of paint. He had been at her building working tirelessly on overdue projects as he tried to get the property back up to his standards. He owned six other buildings, but that one was in the most need of repairs because his uncle didn't do well on the upkeep. If it wasn't for his mother, Bella, making him promise he'd always look after her younger brother Bob before she passed, he would have had a licensed maintenance man there to keep up the property instead of trusting Bob to do the work, because all he did was use the company's card to buy materials for projects he had never gotten around to fixing, and the list was so long for the individual units, it took Omari close to three months before he could get to the major issues.

Realizing that he couldn't pull off the jobs alone, he gave in and hired a few contractors from the company he had when he was partners with his now ex- best friend, Morris Vallinas. He and Morris were thick as thieves at one point. College friends, but that didn't stop Omari from fucking his wife. Truth was, Omari had always had a thing for Victoria. She was sexy as hell and always carried herself like a fucking lady. He never imagined he'd cross any lines with her because he always tried to envision her as a sister. He stayed in his lane and respected his best friend's marriage, until one night Victoria called him crying hysterically on the phone. She begged him to convince Morris to come home because she was so tired of being alone, but Morris at the time was hungry for success like any man would be at the start of the business he was out trying to build. But, Victoria wasn't the type to be alone for long. That night she begged Omari to come over and cried about how she could not spend another night alone in that big ass house without having company or someone to talk to.

Foolishly he went, trying to be a friend to her since Morris had made it clear he couldn't come back to Chicago that night. His only intentions were to keep her company for a little while and talk since he and Morris were like brothers, but that was not how things went down. For one, Omari had a thing for plus-sized women, and Victoria was a full-figured, sophisticated, gorgeous masterpiece and every single time he had laid eyes on her, he admired her. She was portioned well with a little gut and oversized arms and thighs, but she carried herself well. Her face was gorgeous as fuck, and Omari always thought she could be a plus-sized model. It didn't take much persuading for him to handle her that night. They sat out by the pool with soft music and red wine and when Victoria asked him to join her in the hot tub, he resisted at first and insisted he should leave, but when she undressed down to nothing right in front of him, his dick convinced him to stay. He struggled with the thought of what he was doing all of two minutes before he took his best-friend's wife and had his way with her. He fucked her all over Morris' house and when he refused to join her in her bed, they made one of the guest rooms their love nest. Since then, every time Morris left town, and Omari didn't join him, he was in between Morris' wife's thick thighs.

Now, she was pregnant and not sure who was the father because she didn't keep up with shit like she had promised. When she informed Omari, he quickly refuted the possibility of it being him. Most times they used condoms, and he was certain it was not his. He had only touched her twice, maybe three times without a rubber, and he was almost one-hundred percent sure she wasn't carrying his seed.

If Morris would have never intercepted his instant message on Victoria's laptop, he would have never known they were fucking. They would still be married, he and Morris would still be partner's and he'd still be fucking Victoria every chance he got, if she hadn't gotten pregnant. He wasn't ready for any kids, and her getting pregnant only turned him off.

It was truly nothing against Morris. He loved Morris like a brother, but it was something about Victoria. Her body felt good when he held her, and he loved how tight and snug her center was. Only with plus-sized women, Omari felt that way. He had dated a few slim ones, but they never turned him on like a plump, voluptuous woman and when he laid eyes on Legacy, he had to have her. She was pretty as fuck and possessed the right amount of sass he liked in a woman he learned after only five minutes in her presence. When she cried to him about how low down Kenny was and how she was ready to move on, he knew she was as good as his, but then bam, out of the blue she flipped the script and went right back to that sorry ass son of a bitch that she had described as a heartbreaker. He lost her before he made her his own, and he was now even more determined to take her from Kenny because that motherfucker didn't deserve a woman like Legacy. *He* deserved her, and she owned a cat he had to lick. Legacy would be his, and even though she didn't know it, he would have her for himself.

He finished out his day and as luck would have it, Legacy was coming in when he was on his way out. Every day he hoped he would casually run into her, and that day was his lucky day. Legacy had shopping bags in her hand and looked like she could use some help. *A perfect opportunity*, he thought.

He opened the door and held it for her, but she didn't look at him. "Thank you," was all she said and hurried by him without giving him a glance.

"You're welcome, Legacy. It looks like you could use some help," he quickly offered, taking large strides to catch his fast moving target.

"I'm fine, and I got this," she said and kept moving forward. She got to the elevator and struggled to lift her weighed down arm to press the call button.

"I got that," he said and pressed the button for her.

"Thank you," she said, keeping her head straight and her eyes glued on the stainless steel elevator doors. She refused to give him a glance.

"Legacy, you are toting about eight bags, I'll be happy to help you."

She finally shot him a look. "I don't need your help, Omari, and I don't care to even have a conversation with you. You've done enough already, putting idea's in my fiancé's head about what went on between us. I've asked you repeatedly to stop calling my damn phone and texting me. Now, you got Kenny looking at me crazy," she barked and finally, the doors opened. She rushed in, but Omari quickly hopped on. He hit her floor number because she had too many bags in her hand to even press the button. She was stubborn, and he liked that.

"Listen, Legacy, I know my calls and texts have been obsessive, but I was only trying to talk to you. I thought it was inconsiderate of you to hang out with me and then just act as if we hadn't met. I was really digging you, Legacy, and then you just went back to your ex."

"Omari, we hung out like what? Two minutes, and then you come off all stalker-ish and shit. I was digging you too, but we didn't do much of anything to have you all bonkers over me. That shit makes me uncomfortable."

"Look, I'm sorry, okay? I just like you, Legacy. It was messed up that we had such a good time kicking it, and you convinced me that Kenny's ass was black history. You had my nose wide open, and then suddenly you fall back without reason. You could have at least said something."

She softened her stance and dropped the frown from her face. "You know what, Omari, you are right. I should have just told you, but I swear I didn't think a guy like you would even give a damn. I mean, you are gorgeous and successful. I honestly didn't think you'd care."

"Well, you're wrong," he said, and the elevator doors opened. She stepped out, and he offered to help again. "Legacy, let me carry your bags. This is ridiculous. You're sweating, and I know your hands are going to have red bruises after you put those bags down."

"Fine," she gave in, and he took the majority. They got to her unit and even though Omari was sure she shouldn't have, she allowed him to come in.

"Thanks for your help. Those bags were heavy as hell, but I refused to make two trips."

"Anytime, beautiful."

She blushed. "Listen, you should go. If Kenny saw you here, he'd be pissed."

"Yea, I'm sure. I know you love him because he's your kids' dad and all, but when he fucks up again or goes MIA, you know how to get in touch with me," he offered.

"I do, but Kenny and I are good, Omari. And please stop calling and texting. It's causing issues with me and Kenny."

"So, we can't at least be friends?"

"Omari, you know Kenny is not going for that."

"I know, but we can keep it between us. Hanging out is no harm. I know you're with him, Legacy," he continued to lay on the charm.

Legacy looked down and then back up at him. "Maybe, okay? I had fun spending time with you, so maybe."

"Maybe is better than no," he accepted and headed towards the door, and then he stopped. "I hope Kenny realizes what he has."

"He does, Omari. That's why he proposed. He chose me this time."

"For now," Omari said without giving Legacy a chance to respond. He was out the door and down the hall. He had plans to get what he wanted. Before long, Legacy would be calling on him to rescue her from the pains of Kenny when he breaks her heart. From what she had told him about Kenny, Omari was certain of that shit. He just had to be a little patient.

Chapter Seven
Legend Morgan

"No problem, sis. They can stay the night," Legend told his sister, Legacy. She called and told him that Kenny was doing a double and that she had gotten a last minute sew-in. Their mother was the primary care person for the baby, and Kierra had to be picked up by seven from after school care. That sometimes put Legacy in a crunch because even though the center had extended their hours to seven that year, Legacy still made it at seven-fifteen and on her worst days, seven-thirty. Legend, Legacy's older brother, had two teenaged twin girls and one eight-year-old daughter who were best friends with her cousin, Kierra. Legend adored children and since their mother was approaching her mid-sixties, Legend never had a problem picking up his nieces if he had to.

He was a mechanic and owned three shops, so his hours were flexible. Legend was always Legacy's back-up and superhero brother on the days she and Kenny just couldn't make it, because his hours belonged to him. He wasn't a shift worker, and he was a life saver if you asked any other person on this planet. If you asked his wife, she'd say he was a pushover and a half-ass man. She had no more love or respect for him, and he knew it but he still stayed. He didn't want to hurt his kids, nor did he want to have to fight over assets.

Legend and Jacqueline had been married sixteen years, but the last three had been hell for the two of them. She made time for everything and everybody, except him. He would plan romantic evenings only for her to complain during the entire dinner or outing. He would leave her gifts, but she stopped saying thank you or even rewarding him with a simple kiss or hug. It took him at least five or six attempts to get her on the phone if he called, and if it wasn't money or children related, she never rushed to answer a text message. The sex was non-existent, and at times Legend wondered why she even bothered to stay when he knew deep down she wanted to leave.

After making sure the younger girls were down and reminding his twins, Mia and Tia, to not be up all night, he headed downstairs. The kitchen was a mess because they made homemade pizzas, so he got to work. Finally, there was no music coming from upstairs, so he figured the twins had obliged his wishes to not stay up late, so he made a drink and settled on the sofa in their family room. After a bit of channel surfing, he finally settled on *Law & Order*. It was still one of his favorites, so he overlooked the fact that he had seen that episode before. By the fourth rerun and third drink, he realized it was close to 1:00 in the morning, and Jacqueline hadn't found her way home yet. He thought to call her, but that would have been a waste and texting her would only keep him stalking his iPhone for a response. He decided to do neither and went to the bar and fixed another scotch on the rocks. He looked around his massive family room open to the kitchen and formal dining room and wished the lady of his house wanted to be there.

He afforded his family the best of everything because he was a great mechanic and had a strong head for business. Their father died when he was nineteen, leaving his first shop to his family and with that, school took a backseat. Legend was always good with his hands, and his father had taught him everything there was to know about cars, foreign and domestic. His mom wanted to sell the shop, but Legacy and

Legend wouldn't hear of it. Since their father left the shop solely to his son, there was nothing their mother could do to stop Legend from dropping out of college and working at the shop full-time.

It didn't take him long to increase the business, and the money started to overflow which opened the opportunity for another location. Determined and driven, he had his third location five years after that, and he lived well. He provided his family with the best of the best and didn't understand why Jacqueline had just thrown in the towel. Legend was a stud. He was six foot five and had his father's dark complexion, but the same hazel eyes as Legacy. They had both inherited that feature from their mother. He didn't have the same washboard abs he owned a couple of years ago, but there was no flab on his fit waist. With broad shoulders and an easy smile, Legend often wondered why he stayed or even gave two fucks about Jacqueline.

"What-the-fuck-ever," he spat and quickly polished off his glass. He glanced at his watch and then reached for the Johnny Walker black bottle again. "Last one, my friend, and take it to bed," he told himself. He put more than a shot into his glass, and then he heard the garage. She was home. He walked over to the kitchen island and stared at the door. Finally, she came in.

"You're still up?" she said when she sauntered through the kitchen door.

"Yep, and you're home late again."

"I was working?" she defended and put her purse, keys and phone on the island.

"Working on what at this hour, Jackie?" he inquired. She looked so fucking sexy in her dress and pumps, and he knew damn well she wasn't at the fucking office that late dressed like that.

"Legend, please. Must we do this? I've had a long day, and I'm too tired to argue tonight."

His voice was mellow and calm. "Jacqueline, I don't want to fight or argue with you. I just want to know where you been. You come strolling in at this hour when you've been gone since eight this morning. We have three children," he reminded her.

"I see we have five tonight, since I see Kennedy's damn diaper bag again!" she grumbled.

"You don't have to look after my nieces. I've never put that responsibility on you."

"But they are always here!" she shrieked.

"How the fuck would you know?" he yelled back. "You are never fucking here. I need to know what in the fuck is going on with you? What in the fuck is going on with us? We are not who we used to be, and I need to know how to fucking fix it, or we need to find another way," he declared.

"Another way, another way, what do you mean another way," she rushed over to him.

"You are doing somebody, and it's not me. If you don't want this, we have to end this marriage. I can't go another motherfucking day like this."

"Legend, baby, please don't talk like that. I don't want out. There is no one else. I don't want to end this!" she cried.

"Then give me my wife back!" He downed his drink, slammed the glass onto the counter and left the room. He went into their master, and she came in moments later. She walked close to him while he undressed.

"I'm sorry, and I'm here," she said and caressed his chest. She kissed his chest, and his dick grew hard. She hadn't touched him in months. He couldn't help himself because he was hungry for her. He wasn't a cheating man, and he normally relieved himself with porn and lubricant, but that night he wanted to feel the heat of her pussy. He wanted her tight walls nestled around his pole, and he wasn't going to turn down that moment to feel his wife's insides. He grabbed her face and pushed his tongue down her throat. His dick throbbed so hard against his jeans he had to free himself, so he used one hand to unbuckle his pants.

He pushed the top of his jeans and the boxer band under his erection. "Suck it for me, Jackie. Please suck my dick the way you used to."

She stared him in the eyes with a look of sincerity and then dropped to her knees and took him inside of her mouth. Not having the sensation of her tongue and wet hot mouth on his manhood in so long, his body betrayed him, and he shot hot nut in her mouth within moments of her deep throating his dick. He wasn't embarrassed because she knew how long it had been since she had even touched him. "Take off your clothes," he groaned.

"Baby, you just came," she cried, and he could have sworn he heard panic in her voice.

"I know, but I want to fuck you tonight, and I'm not taking no for an answer!" he growled. He was hungry for her. He wanted to taste her, stroke her and make love to her.

"Let's shower first, baby. I've been working all day," she refuted.

He saw the panic on her face as she said those words. There it was. It was the look of a cheating bitch that needed to wash the other motherfucker away from her body before doing him. He just nodded and said, "After you," and followed her into the shower. They both lathered, and he got out before she did. He knew she wanted time to double scrub her pussy, but he was all right with that.

When she finally climbed into bed, he decided not to lick the place he knew another man had invaded, but he ravished her lips, neck and nipples. When he entered his wife's body, he knew he hadn't been the only one there. She felt good, no doubt, but not snug enough for her to have been celibate for all those months she wasn't fucking him. He worked her over and put her to sleep and then laid there in the dark with his eyes to the ceiling. He was hurt. It was time to cut her ass loose, but his heart ached because he still loved her. The tears rolled from his eyes and landed in his ears as he tried to comfort himself enough to fall asleep. She turned over and laid on his chest, not seeing him crying in the dark. "I love you, Legend," she said and held onto him tight.

He wrapped his arms around her and kissed the top of her head. "I love you too."

Chapter Eight

Mia

Mia looked at her phone and wished he would stop calling. She was tired of his attempts to see her. Although she was having the time of her life with Morris, Rene was always on her mind. “Fuck, fuck, fuck, stop calling me!” she blasted.

“Who is that, baby?” Morris asked. She didn’t know he had come home. She didn’t hear him enter the room.

She looked up from her phone into his gorgeous eyes and lied. “It’s my ex roommate, Nicole. She is calling me about girl’s night. I already told her I’d get back to her when I know what the solid plans are, but she keeps blowing up my phone.”

“Well, why don’t you pick up and just talk to her? She could be calling for something else.”

If Mia’s words were true, she knew he’d be right, but she continued with her lie. “Nah, I know that’s what it is because when I texted her she told me to call her. Don’t you hate that?” she said and swiped her screen and hit delete. She didn’t want Morris to see her new name for Rene, which was now *Fuck Boy*, on her screen.

“Yeah, I do, but sometimes the things you have to say are way too much to text. Sometimes it’s easier to just talk.”

“I guess you’re right, but I’ll call her back later. I really don’t want to talk about girl’s night right now because not everyone is on the same page, so the conversation would be pointless,” she huffed. He walked closer to her. After giving her a quick kiss, he moved over to the dresser to remove his watch. “So, what brings you home so early? I thought you had a meeting with that doctor to discuss renovating his office?"

"I did, but he had an emergency with one of his patients, so we had to reschedule. I'm all yours now," he smirked while he unbuttoned his shirt and undid his belt.

"And why are you taking off your clothes?"

"Why aren't you taking off yours?" he countered.

"Because it's like two in the afternoon," she laughed. He moved closer to her and caressed her face. She looked up at him and smiled. "Okay, okay, okay. I guess a little love in the afternoon won't hurt," she grinned. As soon as she was down to her thongs, Morris was licking her clit and twisting her nipples, just the way Mia liked. She arched her back while his tongue stroked her and moaned softly. She opened wider for him and held his head in place as she slow rolled her body against his mouth. She loved the sweet sensations he gave her, and as soon as she closed her eyes, there he was again, stupid ass Rene. Mia wanted to concentrate on Morris, but Rene's two-timing ass was playing a love scene in her mind. No matter how good Morris treated her and made her feel, she couldn't get Rene out of her damn mind or heart. "Oh, baby, suck that clit, baby. Make that pussy cum," she moaned. With that, she held onto his head tighter and lifted her bottom from the bed, giving him all of her. She wanted to release so she could stop thinking of the other fucking no good ass man. "Morris, baby, oh shit, oh shit, Morris!" she screamed, forcing her thoughts on the man devouring her center.

"Cum for me, baby," he hissed and then sucked her bulb. "Cum so I can slide this dick into your wet ass pussy," he coached. He pushed his tongue against her swollen clit again and hit her spot just right, and then she released.

"Ahhh shit, oooh fuck, baby. That was so good. You are so good, baby," she panted. He gently kissed her lower lips and then planted sweet kisses on her inner thighs.

"Can I feel you now, baby?" Morris whispered.

"Yes, baby, yes. Give me that dick, baby. Fuck me with that big ass dick," she added, knowing she was pushing it. His dick was far from big, but at that moment she wanted him, all of him anyway. She rolled onto her side and lifted her leg. She missed that position and couldn't wait for him to slide in. He got behind her and made every attempt he could to fuck her in that position, her favorite position, but his dick kept slipping out. *You gotta be fucking kidding me*, Mia thought to herself, pissed the fuck off as she pressed her ass against him trying to help him find his way back inside, but it was a wasted attempt. She tried not to show her frustration, but he knew she wasn't happy with how shit was going down.

She rolled over onto her back, and he got on top. She spread her legs as wide as she could to give him access and once he found his rhythm, it made her moan. It was decent, definitely not horrible, but damn sure not the big dick she was accustomed to from king ding-a-ling Rene. He sped up and pumped her short and hard, and she moaned because it felt good. It felt so good that she came again and cheered him on until he came. Both were out of breath and stared into each other's eyes.

"You feel so good, baby, and I'm sorry," he said.

"What for?" she asked.

"For you know..."

"Morris, baby, please. Did you not just feel my pussy erupt for you? You have nothing to be sorry about. Come here," she said and held out her arms, and he rested on top of her.

"I know I ain't packing, and if this is going to be a problem, please let's end this now because I'm falling so hard or you."

"And I'm also falling hard for you, Morris. I am not sprung, but I'm definitely turned on and always satisfied every time you do me, so please don't keep bringing up your dick. I'm here, aren't I?"

He kissed her lips. "Yes, and you are special to me. I hope we can go all the way."

"You already know that you want to go all the way with me?" she asked. With Rene that had been music to her ears, but now it sounded different. More like she was settling. Why did the size of the dick matter? It was good and made her cum, but it wasn't the explosiveness she shared with Rene. She questioned her sanity and wondered why Rene was still a factor when Morris was perfect.

"I'm not one-hundred percent certain, but I have a good feeling about us."

She smiled. "So do I." She wasn't one-hundred percent confident in her words, but she knew she wanted to be happy and a man's wife, not his side piece. If she could get that from Morris she'd win because besides the fact of his tiny dick, everything else about that man was noteworthy.

He got up from the bed and extended a hand to her. "Now, come and let's clean up and go get something to eat."

"No, baby, I want a nap," she whined and pulled the covers over her body.

He leaned in to give her another soft kiss. "Fine, you can take a nap, but not a long one. I'm starving, and I want to take you out to some place nice."

"Like you always do," she smiled. He headed for the bathroom and as soon as he was on the other side of the door, her smile faded. He was so sweet and picture-perfect, so why was she stuck on stupid ass Rene? Why couldn't she get that motherfucker and his anaconda dick out of her head? "If I could only feel his dick one more time. Just let him bite my nipples and let me ride his face," she mumbled and then punched the pillow. "Damn you, Rene!" she snarled. She shut her eyes tight, and since it was impossible to stop missing him and thinking of him, she let thoughts of him dance around her head until she fell asleep.

Chapter Nine

Kenny

Kenny sat outside and waited for Tanya to close up shop. He didn't want to be alone with her, but he had to have a one-on-one with her ass. Still unable to believe she was pregnant by him, he thought it would be best if they took a trip to the drugstore and got a new test. He had to see it to believe it, so if that meant him standing in the doorway while she pissed on that stick, that's what it would be. When he saw her come out and put her key into the lock, he tapped his horn to get her attention. She looked his way, and he waved. Even though he wasn't standing right in front of her, he knew she rolled her eyes. She finished locking up and then walked in his direction with rapid stone cold attitude strides. It was written all over her face and confirmed when she got up on his door.

"Kenny, what in the fuck are you doing here? We were supposed to meet tomorrow for lunch, remember?"

"True, but I got this sinking feeling in the pit of my stomach that I just can't shake, so we need to hit up this Walgreens, grab a test and you need to piss for me."

"Are you fucking serious!" she shrieked.

"Dead fucking serious," he blasted back.

"Get the fuck outta here, Kenny. I gave you the ultrasound pictures. I ain't about to piss on no stick in front of yo' ass like I'm some lying, home wrecking side chick," she snapped with a hand on one hip and her designer purse resting in the crook of her other arm.

"LaTanya, I'm not calling you out on your intentions. I don't give a fuck about none of that shit. All I want to do is know for sure that you are pregnant."

She laughed out loud and looked up into the air like an answer would fall from the sky. "Kenny, I gave you the damn sonogram!"

"And that shit can be printed from the internet. So, if you're really fucking pregnant, come hit up this Walgreens with me, get a test and we go to your place so you can piss for me. It's so fucking simple, LaTanya. If you can't do that, I'll kindly ask that you stay the fuck away from me and my family."

"Yo' family? Yo' motherfucking family?" she spat with hand gestures. "Gon' with that bullshit. Your motherfucking family wasn't a priority when you were dipping into my pussy every chance you got behind Legacy's back, were they? How 'bout I call Legacy and tell her that shit since you try to play like you a motherfucking family man now! Did you tell Legacy you were eating this pussy way back when she was pregnant with that last baby of yours?" she challenged. For a moment, Kenny had nothing to say because the words she spoke were true. He had hooked up with Tanya behind Legacy's back, and Legacy thought they hooked up after he moved out.

"Man, fuck all that shit. I was dead wrong back then for the bullshit I was doing, but what matters now is the here and fucking now. Legacy knows everything that went down with us," he lied. He didn't want her to think she had shit else on him. "I told her everything when I went back to her," he continued to lie and that shut Tanya up fast. "So like I said, if you want to see my face again, we gon' take a test."

She stood for a few seconds looking at him in disbelief. "You told Legacy everything, and she still let you come back?"

"Legacy and I are good now. Better and stronger than we ever were, and ain't shit you could tell her that would change that."

She wasn't convinced. "You told her you were in Atlantic City with me the night she went into labor with Kennedy?"

Kenny sighed. "I told her everything," he said with a straight face. He was lying his ass off, but it had to be done so she would take the test and keep her mouth closed. Now, there was nothing to hide, so Tanya was out of bullets.

"Fine!" she snapped and rolled her neck and eyes. "I'll meet you at my house. Get the damn test!"

He watched her strut to her vehicle and didn't pull off until she pulled away. Rehashing the past, he grimaced. Kenny then wished he had come clean and told Legacy everything, but he hadn't. No way would she have let him back if she knew the truth about him and Tanya. When he moved in with Tanya, she promised she would never tell Legacy when they started messing around, but now since he was marrying her, he knew his secret might not stay a secret for long. If Tanya was in fact pregnant, he had to keep the peace between the two of them because he knew Tanya would mention something just to throw it in Legacy's face.

After he picked up the tests, he headed to Tanya's. Something inside of him was a little excited, and he was also scared. He didn't know what he would do if she was having his baby, but he would love that kid just as much as he loved the other two. He parked and headed up towards the porch, and Tanya quickly opened the door for him.

"What took you so long, Kenny?"

"I wasn't sure which one I should get, so I got three different ones," he said and then stretched out his hand to give her the bag.

She snatched it. "Well, you took so damn long, I pissed already."

"Bullshit, Tanya. I took what, all of fifteen fucking minutes!"

"Yeah, and I couldn't hold it."

"So we wait," he said, unzipping his coat.

"You're kidding me right?"

"Do I fucking look like I'm kidding?" he asked and headed up the steps. She shut the door and followed him up to the kitchen. He pulled out a stool and sat at the peninsula.

"Do you want a beer?" she offered.

"Sure, and you need to pour yourself a tall glass of water or juice so you can go."

"Relax, Kenny, damn! I'll piss on your stupid little pregnancy test so you can go home to your kids and your fat ass fiancée," she spat and slammed the fridge door.

"Listen, Tanya, you have to chill with the name calling and disrespect. It's childish, and if we are going to raise this kid together, you have to do better. You're a grown ass woman talking like you're a fucking twelve-year-old girl."

"Oh, so I can be bitches and whores, but Legacy can't be fat? As a matter of fact, a fat bitch, how about that!" she shot him and then popped the top on his beer.

"Nope, not cool, so chill on that shit. Why do you hate Lay so much? I mean, what the fuck has she done to you, Tanya? Y'all were cool back in the day, and when y'all were in hair school, y'all were even tighter. We are the ones who did foul shit to Legacy, not the other way around, so why do you hate her so damn much?"

She slid the beer in his direction. "I don't hate Legacy. I just can't stand her smart-ass mouth. She thinks she can just say what the fuck she wants when she wants, and that's what I can't stand about her. We hooked up, yes, and we were wrong, but she fucking stopped talking to me, but kept fucking yo' trifling ass."

"Tanya, we have kids together. She can't just write me off like she did you. And as fucked up as it all was, Legacy and I have something that I didn't have with you."

"What?"

"Real love," he answered.

"Ha!" she yelled. "That bullshit ain't real. If it were, you would have never fucked around with me. You would have never left her for me."

"I didn't leave her for you. I left because I was too damn busy chasing what looked like gold. Let's just be real for a minute or two, Tanya. Your ass jumped through hurdles to have me. Was on your best behavior, fucking me right, sucking my dick on command, but once you got me it became all about you, and your stuck-up ass forgot how to treat me right. The difference is, you dropped the ball, but Legacy has always been on my team and has never even fumbled the fucking ball. I was a stupid, dumb ass idiot when I hooked up with you. I thought the grass was greener, but it was all dried up and dead."

"Fuck you, Kenny! If it wasn't for this baby inside of me, I wouldn't have one motherfucking word to say to your tired ass. I didn't drop the fucking ball, I just got tired of serving a broke ass motherfucker like you with no damn ambition. I am going somewhere, Kenny, and all you want is that blue-collar life. I got goals and ambitions, and I thought you had them too. Back when we used to fuck around, you used to tell me how you wanted to open your own business as a computer technician, and you'd brag about calling your chain Dr. Keys, but once we made our thing official, you became content with the mill. You never talked about going back to school to get your degree.

"We never talked about you starting a business and when I'd mention it, you'd find a humorous way to change the subject, so my grass ain't dried up, baby. It's plush and green, but you'll never cut it again. Now, where is the damn test so I can piss and you can go home to your fake ass family!"

He gave a point to the other counter. She snatched the bag and headed toward the bathroom. "Oh no, you women are slick as fuck. I need to watch you piss. Knowing you, there are positive sticks under the cabinet."

"Whatever, Kenny," she mumbled. He followed closely and stood in the doorway while she dropped her yoga pants and sat. "Hand me a cup," she said and pointed to the disposable Dixie cups on the sink. He gave it to her, and she went. She sat the cup on the counter, opened each kit, dipped them one by one, replaced the cap, washed her hands and then vacated the bathroom. Kenny stood there and watched as all the tests turned positive. She was pregnant, now the question was, was it really his? "Fuck!"

Chapter Ten

Anika

NeNe was in Jaxson's kitchen cooking dinner. She felt more like the lady of the house than just a house guest and wished she had left gay ass Rey long ago and not allowed him to play her for all those years. Strange how she still loved Rey and thought of him often, but he was no fucking good for her. She was not only glad that she had moved on, she was proud that she could resist the urge to answer his unwanted calls. He still texted, and she still didn't reply. Why he still made any attempts were beyond her imagination, and she hoped he got the message and stopped.

She diced the veggies for the salad while she bobbed her head to the best of New Edition. Since she and Jaxson had watched the miniseries on BET, she had New Edition in her daily music rotation. She went back to the fridge to get the cucumbers, and before she took a quick sip of her Merlot, she sang loud and off key to Johnny Gill's verse in *Can You Stand The Rain*. She went back to her salad while she continued to butcher the songs playing from Jaxson's wireless speakers.

A few moments later, she heard the garage door and glanced at the clock. Jaxson said he'd be home late because his schedule ran late, so she guessed one of his showings didn't show or rescheduled. She heard the door open but didn't turn in that direction as she verbally greeted him. "Welcome home, baby. I thought you'd be late."

"Anika?" The female voice called out with surprise.

Shocked, she spun around to see Jaxson's soon to be ex-wife, Michelle. "What are you doing here?" NeNe asked, holding her chest with one hand and her knife in the other.

"Me?" Michelle hissed. "I should be asking you the same damn thing since you're here cooking and all."

"I'm here because I am a guest. I was invited," NeNe snarled, but then loosened the grip she had on the knife. She had met Michelle on a few occasions at office parties and her visits to the office and company picnics.

"Well, I didn't expect anyone to be here. Especially not you. *And* you're cooking? When did this start?"

"No disrespect, Michelle, but I don't owe you an explanation. Does JT even know you're here?"

She dropped her keys in her purse and then shot NeNe a look. "JT? Since you two are on a personal level now, he told me it was okay to come by and grab a few boxes that I left behind from the garage."

"Okay," NeNe said and put down the knife and then folded her arms. "If your business is in the garage, why are you in here?"

"I came in to hit the little girl's room. I had no idea anyone was here. JT told me he'd be late."

"Well, you know where the toilet is. I suggest you handle that and leave," NeNe ordered. She didn't know what came over her, but she became territorial. She was fucking Jaxson now, pleasing his dick, cooking his meals and cleaning his house. She was the one making sure he had a smile on his face 24/7, and this ex piece of trash needed to be gone.

"Excuse me, I will," she shot back and went to the powder room on the main floor. NeNe went back to preparing her dinner and after a few moments, Michelle reappeared.

"Does Jaxson know you still have a key?"

"He may. I mean, I didn't exactly give them back. I still have the garage door opener if that's your next question."

"No, I have no more questions for you, Michelle. I'd like you to go."

"Putting me out, like this is your shit?" she giggled. "NeNe, you have a lot to learn." She headed to the door. "I know there is no need to ask you to tell Jaxson I was here, so until next time," she said and sauntered out. As soon as she shut the door, NeNe went for her phone. She called Jaxson, but he didn't answer.

Call me ASAP! she text.

She tossed her phone and tried to get back to making their dinner, but she was all over the place. She couldn't concentrate and wondered what was delaying his call, so she called him again and again and again. After thirty minutes of unanswered calls and texts, she forced herself to finish making dinner. She didn't want her money to go to waste on the things she had purchased, and if she had to pack it up and take it with her, she would. An hour or so later, he walked through the door. NeNe had already polished off a bottle of wine. She was pissed and declared she would not start her relationship off that way. Rey would be the final man to do her dirty, and Jaxson was on the chopping block.

"Hey, baby," he said, leaning in to kiss her cheek. She guessed he didn't notice the frown she was wearing because he moved about the kitchen as if all was good. "It smells so damn good in here, baby, and your man is starving," he said, peeping into the pots on the stove. It took him a few moments to realize she wasn't herself. "Baby, what is it? What's wrong?" he asked, rushing over to her side.

She put her head down. "I called and text and called and text," she mumbled.

"I'm sorry, but I left my phone at the office. It was late, and I didn't go back to get it. I'm sorry, honey," he explained and then gave her another kiss.

"Why does Michelle still have a key to your place?" she asked. He was going for the fridge, but he paused and looked at her confused. "Don't look shocked, Jaxson. I'm so not in the mood to play fucking games with you!" she yelled and leaped from the stool she was sitting on.

"Woe, woe, woe, Anika. Calm down and tell me what's going on?" he demanded. "Michelle was here?"

"Yes, she was, and she just walked in and scared the living shit out of me!"

He grabbed NeNe, but she pulled away. "Listen, I don't know how she still has a key to my place. At the last hearing she was ordered to hand over her copies. Yes, I am sure she has the garage code, she has boxes here, but I had no idea she still had a key."

"Well, she does, and she walked in on me cooking and made it clear that you knew she had a key."

"NeNe, that is bullshit, and you know it. Why would my fucking soon to be ex-wife still have keys to my home? You've been here with me, and you know damn well if that was the case I wouldn't have you here all up in my damn bed. Come on now, baby, think. Ever since the break-up, I've opened my heart and home to you. Why would I do that if I had something going on with Michelle? She had no damn business coming up in here, and I'm going to set this shit straight right now!" He patted his pockets for his phone. "Oh fuck, baby. My phone is at the office."

"How fucking convenient."

He pulled her back into his strong arms. "I'm not a liar. I've never lied to you. Michelle and I talk, and I've been there for her since her mother has been battling this cancer, but you know that is it, NeNe. I tell you when and where, I don't lie to you."

She gazed into his eyes. They were sincere, unlike Rey's, and she had to stop comparing him to Rey. She had to stop dropping him in that category every single time things were off.

"I'm not him. I know you are scared, and your heart is frail. I won't hurt you, Anika. You are so fucking special to me and for the first time in my life, I miss a woman when I'm not with her. I mean, you are the first woman I miss. You invade my thoughts no matter what I'm thinking or what I'm doing, and you don't have a thing to worry about. Michelle is my past, and my future is standing right here in front of me, but you have to learn how to trust again. Once you have learned how to do that, episodes like this will never arise again in this relationship."

She sighed. "I'm trying, but it's like as soon as I relax, shit is right back at me. Do you know how it made me feel when she just strolled in the door?"

"I can only imagine, and I am sorry. I will handle Michelle and change the locks, whatever it takes for you to trust me."

She nodded, and he kissed her. He grabbed her ass, and she wrapped her legs around his waist. Soon after, his dick was stroking her as he held her up against the pantry door. That was the first time they had fucked without a condom, and Jaxson's dick felt like platinum as he pushed his pipe to the hilt. She felt his head bang against her cervix and cried out his name. She experienced pleasure and pain, and her emotions were on high because she felt like Jaxson was the one.

He told her play-by-play of his day. If he was going to Michelle's, he told her. He never lied to her, and she had to put on her big girl panties and handle Michelle like a real woman instead of a coward like she had been earlier that evening. She should have demanded that Michelle leave the key, but she was the newcomer, the new woman, and that was Jaxson's job, not hers. She just had to trust that he was the real deal and when he pulled out, went down on his knees and put her thighs over his shoulders, she stopped thinking about Rey, Michelle and the rest of the world. He licked her pussy so good she forgot her own name. When her pussy contracted, she held his crania tightly in place and rolled her hips. She creamed so damn good, she screamed like she was being murdered.

When he finally released her, she ordered him over to the sofa so she could ride him, but he declined and made her bend over on the stairs. He pushed his pipe in one quick thrust and pumped short and hard until he erupted. He held her hips tightly, digging into her flesh and growled loud enough to signal the dogs and coyotes in the neighborhood. Knowing she pleased him so well gave her a sense of pride. Like all women, she loved when a man enjoyed her pussy, and the sounds that came out of Jaxson were validation that Michelle was no competition and definitely not a threat.

Chapter Eleven

Legacy

Things had been quiet for the most part after Kenny confirmed that Tanya's pregnancy wasn't a hoax. Deep down, Legacy wished Tanya was lying but since she wasn't, she had to figure out a way to cope with it because the shit had her feeling dejected. She was depressed and angry, but she tried to not show it at home. She knew Kenny hadn't planned it, but she was so mad at him, and every little thing he did irritated the fuck out of her. She didn't want to be that way with Kenny, but she couldn't help it. She wished he could undo what he had done.

She finished cleaning her station and like the last few evenings, she was the last one to leave. She locked the door to the shop and walked towards her car and was shocked to see Omari in the parking lot.

"What are you doing here?" Legacy questioned with a hand on her hip. She was not happy to see his ass.

"I was in the area and dropped by to say hey."

"Really, Omari? You just happened to be on this side of town?"

"Yes," he answered and walked up to her. "You see that building right over there?" he said and pointed.

"Yes," Legacy replied with a nod.

"That building is up for sale, and I'm thinking about buying it."

"That run-down ass building?"

"Yes. That run-down building is in a prime neighborhood, and it is priced good. With a little work," he paused and then chuckled.

"Correction, with a lot of work, it could very well be a great investment."

She gazed at it. "I can only imagine. This is a good location. If I lived this close to work, I'd be able to walk."

"Well, if I buy it and rehab it, you could be one of my first tenants," he smiled.

"Why are you so fucking charming, Omari?"

"I'm just being myself."

"Yes, your charming self," she said. He just looked at her. "Look, I need to get going. I have to pick up my kids from my brother's house."

"Really? I was hoping you'd have a drink with me."

"Omari, you know better. Why do you keep pursuing me? I'm engaged, and I've told you over and over that you and I can't be hanging out and shit."

"I know, and this is not a pursuit, Legacy. I asked could we just hang and be friends. I know as much as I like you that your mind is made up, so I'll go with a friendship."

Legacy looked around. She needed a breather, and Kenny was on her last nerve. She was so sick of hearing how sorry he was for knocking that bitch Tanya up. "Omari, I don't know if that's a good idea. If Kenny knew I was even talking to you, he'd flip the fuck out."

"As I told you before, this is just between us. I don't kiss and tell," Omari said and hit her with his sexy smirk.

She contemplated again and then sighed. She knew damn well she should have just taken her black ass home, but she gave in.

"Okay. One drink, and it has to be some place in the opposite direction. All of Kenny's friends know me, and I don't need any more drama on top of the baby mama drama we already have," Legacy slipped and said.

"You're pregnant?" Omari asked.

"No, but …," she hesitated, and then said, "But his ex is," Legacy admitted. She had already let it slip, so no point in hiding it. Chicago was big but small, and she was sure Omari would see Tanya's pregnant ass one day in their building waddling with Kenny.

"Word?" He looked surprised at the news as he should have been. Legacy wasn't broadcasting it, and she had avoided Omari as much as she could.

"Let's get out of here so we can talk," Legacy said. She headed to her car while he got into his truck. They went to a pub not far from the salon where Legacy filled Omari in on what was going on with her and Kenny.

"So what y'all gon' do? Are you still going to marry him?" Omari quizzed. He dipped a chip into the salsa and popped it into his mouth.

"We're dealing with it, and yes, I'm still going to marry him," she answered. "Kenny didn't cheat on me when she conceived. It's just one of those things that happened. She didn't show up until after we got engaged."

"Are you certain?" he asked suspiciously.

Legacy knew he was trying to put doubts in her mind, but she was sure Kenny would never do anything like that to her. To stage a scene with Tanya coming over to announce her news would be too farfetched. "Fuck yes!" she snapped. "Kenny is not that trifling, Omari."

"Well, you said Tanya was someone you once called a friend," he added.

"Yes, I did," she snuffed. "But him hooking up with her didn't shock me. I mean, a ho gon' be a ho, and Kenny was just on some stupid shit at that time. If he had known she was pregnant, he'd have told me, so stop looking at me like that," she snapped.

"Like what?" he grinned.

Legacy wanted to wipe that grin from his fine ass face. "You know what the fuck I'm talking about. That sly ass look you had like I'm being a fool for Kenny, but I'm not. Kenny and I are meant to be, and this baby situation is just another hurdle we have to jump, but we'll be fine."

"All right, all right," he said and took a sip of his beer. "I know you're not stupid, Legacy. And I see that no matter what you trust and love Kenny, so good luck with that situation. As a friend, I'll just wish you well, but know that I'm here if you need a shoulder to cry on."

"I'm good, Omari," she said and took a sip of her wine. They fell silent, and then a guy cleared his throat, getting their attention because neither saw the man approach. Omari didn't seem like he was too happy to see him, and his jaws tightened.

"What do you want, Morris, and why are you at my table?"

"I saw you and thought I'd come over and say hello." The stranger looked at Legacy, but she said nothing. "Allow me to introduce myself," he said to Legacy and extended his hand. "I'm Morris Vallinas, an old friend of Omari's."

"I'm Legacy, nice to meet you," she said, gently shaking his hand.

"Pardon my intrusions, but when I saw my dear friend over here sitting with a lovely young lady like yourself, I wondered if he told you that he has a bad habit of touching things that don't belong to him."

"Morris, that's enough. I need you to get away from my table."

Curious, more like nosey, Legacy asked, "What do you mean?"

"Listen, Legacy, don't listen to shit he says. And Morris, you've said all you had to say the last time I saw you, so please move the fuck on," Omari spoke firmer.

Morris glared at him and then shook his head. "You're right I did, but seeing your ass sitting over here smiling in another woman's face while my pregnant ex-wife keeps calling me for shit that your ass should be handling, pissed me off. Man up and take her calls because I'm not going to take care of your damn kid, so stop ignoring her and go deal with her ass."

"That ain't my damn kid!" Omari huffed.

"We shall see, my friend. She won't be pregnant forever, and DNA don't lie!" Morris snarled. "Take care, my sister, and watch out for this one. He has a bad habit of taking things that don't belong to him."

"Morris, you've said enough!" Omari stood.

Morris didn't budge. "Sit the fuck down because after what you did to me, after you fucked my wife in my got'damn house, trust and believe you don't want none of this," Morris growled. He and Omari stared each other down.

"Omari, please," Legacy sighed. Omari's jaws tightened, and both of his fists were balled up tightly at his side. His light brown complexion was now flushed and red. Legacy hopped off her stool and stood between the two men. "Omari, let's just go," she encouraged.

"No, stay, Miss Legacy," Morris said and straightened his tie. "I'll leave. This is a waste of my time because I'm over it, and I've moved on!" Morris said and then turned and walked away.

Omari cooled his stance. "Sit down," Legacy said softly.

Omari hesitated, but then he snatched the stool from underneath the table and planted himself back onto it. Legacy then climbed back onto her stool. "What was that all about?" Legacy questioned. "Who was that?" Omari took a big gulp of his beer and then sat it back on the table as if Legacy hadn't asked him anything. "Hello," she said. "Are you going to answer me?"

"Leave it alone, Legacy," he responded.

"Oh no, no, no, no, no! I just sat here and told you all of what's going on in my world, so spill it!" she demanded.

He let out a breath. After a few more shorts moments, he said, “That was my ex-partner. He and I had a business together. We’ve been friends since we were in college, but I crossed some lines, had an affair with his wife, and then he found out about it. Shortly after that, we found out she was pregnant. And she’s not sure if I’m the father or if it’s him,” he confessed.

“Get the fuck out of here! You are sitting here judging my man when you’ve done some shit even lower than him!” she spat.

“Listen, Legacy, I know what I did was low,” he sighed.

“You’re got’damn right it was low. That was fucked up, Omari!”

“I know, Legacy. Damn! Fuck, I live with that shit every damn day. This kid thing has me on edge every fucking second of the day. All I do now is bury myself into work and try to focus on something other than that bullshit.”

“So, if you and I would have hooked up, would you have even told me?”

“Of course.”

“Somehow, I find that hard to believe,” she said, going into her purse. She pulled out a twenty and placed it on the table and then stood. “It was real, but I’m out. You’re a piece of work, Omari, and good luck with that situation!” she blasted at him, just like he’d told her.

He jumped up to stop her. “Legacy, wait. Please don’t leave. I have no one to talk to. Everyone in my circle hates me and please … I know it was low, just don’t leave. If I ever needed a friend in my entire life, I need one right now,” he cried. Legacy relaxed her posture and then sat down. “Here,” he said, pushing her twenty back her way. “I’ll pay. I invited you out.”

“Thanks.”

“Thanks for not walking out. I know you don’t owe me shit.”

"You're right, but it looks like you do need a friend, so tell me what happened and what possessed you to fuck another man's wife?"

"Do I have to?"

"If you want me to stay, yes you do!" she declared. With that, he told her everything.

Chapter Twelve

Mia

She closed her eyes and let his tongue trail down from her rock-solid nipples to her navel and then her center. The touch of his tongue made her body tremble, and she grabbed the sheets tightly as if she needed to hold on. She lifted her bottom to push her nectar closer to his mouth, and he took her to the land of pleasure as his tongue stroked her bulb and penetrated her opening.

"Yes, baby, do that shit … You know what I love, baby, please this pussy," she hissed as he went in as deep as he could with his tongue. She pushed her pelvis so far up to his mouth, he replaced his tongue with his fingers and then sucked on her bulb. In a trance, Mia let go, and her orgasm coated his fingers and rolled out of her opening to her asshole, and she felt her own juices lubricate her back hole. "Fuck me in my ass, daddy," she moaned and turned over and positioned herself on the side of the bed.

He didn't hesitate and quickly took his position behind her and grabbed her slender hips. Before he made his way in, he asked, "Are you sure, baby, because I want this pussy so bad," he groaned.

"I want it in my ass, baby. Please make me cum again, and you can have this pussy all night," she said, pressing her ass against his dick. He did as she ordered. He held the side of her waist with one hand and worked his dick from her clit, grazing her center, up her crack and then rubbed his head in a circular motion around her asshole before he pushed himself inside of her. He pushed and pulled and pounded her back end like it was his mission to please her, and she moaned into the pillow she was hugging as she took all of him to the hilt.

"Ahhh, baby, your ass is so tight and good. I'm going to nut, baby. It's so hot and good," he growled. He held onto her tiny waist tight as he pumped harder. She felt his dick growing and her hole stretch wider, and she knew he was about to fill her with his hot cream.

"That's right, baby, fuck that ass. I'm going to cum with you, baby. Fuck it hard, fuck me, Rene! Fuck, fuck, fuck, I'm cumming!" she screamed.

"Oh fuck, oh fuck, Mia baby, you are fucking amazing. I'm cumming, I'm fucking cumming! I missed fucking you, baby, I missed you so fucking much," he grunted. She smiled and panted and as she was about to turn over, she was interrupted.

"Mia, Mia, Mia, wake up," she heard, and her eyes fluttered. She felt someone shake her again. "Mia, wake up." When she fully opened her eyes, she focused on Morris' face. "Were you having a nightmare, baby?"

"Huh, huh, whaaadddd?" she stammered. She couldn't believe it was only a dream. She was just fucked to two of the best orgasms she'd ever had in a damn dream. Instantly, her hand went to her center underneath the covers, and she was soaking wet.

"You were moaning, baby. Were you having a bad dream?" Morris asked again.

"No, No, I, I, I was ummm, I was…Hell, I don't remember what I was dreaming," she lied. "Was I talking in my sleep?" she asked nervously, praying she hadn't said his name.

"No, just the moaning. And you're sweating, baby. What were you dreaming about?"

"I don't know. I think I was running, I honestly can't remember. Can you get me some water please?" she asked.

"Sure, of course," he said and hurried out of the room.

Once he was on the other side of the door, she sat straight up. "Fuck, Rene, why are you in my dreams? Why can't I get over your ass? Why does my body crave you so bad when you're no fucking good for me?" she questioned and then stopped talking to herself when she heard Morris' footsteps coming back down the hall. When he entered the room, she reached out for the bottle of water. "Thank you so much, baby. My throat is super dry."

"It's no problem, honey," he said and then took a seat near her feet. "Are you okay? Lately, things have been a little distant between us, and we haven't made love in days."

"Baby, I am fine. I'm just a little stressed with work. Since Denise has been out on maternity leave, I've been doing a share of her work load, but I'm fine," she said after coating her throat with the cool beverage. She put the bottle down on the nightstand and then reached for his hands. "I'm in the mood now, if you want to," she smiled. That dream had her wet and ready. He stood and leaned in to kiss her.

"I'm always ready to please you, baby. Lay back," he smirked. He got back into bed and then slid under the covers with her and caressed her skin gently. It felt nice, but she wanted him to fuck her, not make love to her. Her nipples ached to be bitten, pinched and twisted, not sucked and gently rubbed.

"Harder, Morris, suck harder, baby," she pleaded. She wanted another dose of the fucking he had put on her the first night when he had her biting the damn covers, but since that night he acted as if he couldn't bring it. He became this passionate 'take your time' type of lover, and Mia loved *back breaking, oh my god* sex. She also loved anal, but he wasn't into it.

"Oh, your pussy is soaking, baby," he said when he kissed her lower lips.

"I know, baby, so suck all my juices and make me cum all over the sheets," she ordered and placed her hands on his head to give him a little push. She wanted him to bury his face in the place and lap up every drop of her love juices. "Yes, baby, yes, yes, yes, umm, yessss," she moaned because he was getting the job done, but all she could think about was Rene. She went up on her elbows to watch him and to focus on the man she was with, but Rene was tugging at her thoughts. She wished it were him sucking and licking her nectar. She still wanted him, still craved him, and she hated herself because Morris was the cream of the crop, a *single* woman's dream.

He was smart, successful and romantic as fuck. Morris opened doors, sent flowers and cooked. He always complimented her as a man should and showed her how a woman was supposed to be treated, but she was still stuck on the two-timing, heart-breaking bastard with a wife and two kids. Morris made surprise visits to her office with lunch and took her on weekend getaways with no lies and drama, but something inside of her wanted Rene so bad that she couldn't enjoy the thing she had going on with Morris. She felt guilty and worried she'd call out Rene's name. She was so twisted, and she wished she could stop and get over Rene's stupid ass, but it was like mission impossible.

Working with him made things worse because she saw him every day. He constantly called and texted her, and she just wanted him to disappear so she could get on with her life.

Momentarily focusing on the man who had her hood pinned back with one hand while he ravished her bulb and fingered her with what she figured were three of his masculine fingers, her head flung back as she rolled her narrow hips into his tongue and fingers, and she exploded. "That feels so fucking good baby, oh my gawwwddd, that is so fucking good!" she hollered. "Ah-ha, ah-ha, ahhh, baby!

That felt so damn good," she released. He came up and kissed every inch of her on his way up to her lips. She threw her arms around his neck. "That was so good, baby, I feel so relaxed now. I want you to fuck this pussy until I cum again and again," she moaned into his mouth between kisses. She was on fire, and she hoped Morris would put out her flame that night and leave her thoroughly satisfied.

"Open wide for me, baby," he whispered, and she obliged. He slid inside of her, and she missed that little sting she used to feel when Rene would push his way inside of her. She didn't get that feeling when Morris entered her body, and she wanted it back so fucking bad that she clenched her muscle every time he penetrated her. He began to pump, and it felt good, but Mia wanted more. She wanted her pussy to ache with pain and pleasure on every stroke. She wanted him deeper and harder, and she wanted to be pounded like a chef tenderizing a piece of meat. It felt nice, like she knew he was there, but she wanted to be filled with a man-sized piece of pipe, not a boy-sized pole. She moaned softly and tried to make herself cum with him penetrating her, but no matter how much she clenched and squeezed her core, he couldn't get her there.

She interrupted him mid-stroke. "Let me turn over, baby. Can you hit it from the back?" she requested.

"Yasssss, baby, turn that ass over so I can fuck that pussy right," he grumbled. She fought the urge to roll her eyes and turned over to get on all fours. She wished he'd slide his dick into her ass. She pressed her ass into him, hoping it would slip into her ass so he'd see how good it felt. His dick was just perfect for anal because it wasn't big enough to burn, but it would do its duty of giving her a hard orgasm.

"Slow down, baby, hold on. I can't get it in with you rolling your ass like that."

"Yes you can, baby, just slide it right on in my ass, and I promise you'll love it," she hissed and continued to squirm, trying to get it in the hole she wanted it to be in. He instantly backed away. She looked over her shoulders at him. "What, baby, what's wrong?"

"Why do you keep asking me to do that? I told you I don't get down like that. Why in the fuck do you keep pushing it!" he thundered.

"Morris, damn, okay baby, don't…Stop, okay? Let's continue making love, baby. I'm sorry," she cried. He didn't budge at first, and then he got into the bed and laid back on the pillow and rested his arms behind his head. "Look, I'm sorry, please," she said, moving closer to him. She laid her head on his stomach.

He rubbed her head. "I know you're used to other shit with other men you've been with, Mia. A bigger dick, kinky shit and getting fucked in the ass, but I'm not down with it, and I wish you'd stop asking." That time he sounded dead ass serious.

She wondered what was wrong with it, so she asked because she hadn't always been too fond of it either. Rene was a master at fucking, and once he showed her the way to painless anal sex, she was hooked on it. "Why is it such a horrible idea, Morris? Truthfully, I wasn't always an anal fan, but once I tried it, I've grown to love it. All I'm asking you is to at least try it. I know you'll enjoy it."

"No!" he roared.

Her head popped up from his stomach, and she looked at him. She had never heard that tone from him. He jumped up from the bed and went to the bathroom and slammed the door. She sat in his bed in the dark and wondered what the fuck had just happened. When he finally came back to bed, the mood was gone, and Mia had already gotten under the covers on the side of the bed she now owned. He got into the bed and turned his back to her which was something foreign to Mia because Morris had never treated her that way. He was cold, like another side of him that she didn't want to get to know.

"Can we at least talk about it?" she pleaded.

"Good night, Mia," he replied.

"Morris, baby," she touched his back.

"Good night, Mia," he said again, his voice deep and firm.

Mia drew back her arm, moved back to her side of his Cal King bed and pulled up the covers. She decided to leave it alone. It took a few minutes, but eventually she fell asleep. The next morning when she got up, he was already gone. After she showered and dressed for work, she went downstairs where his housekeeper, Magdalene, had her breakfast ready. Normally, Morris would leave a note with Magdalene who would hand it to her as soon as she sat, or she'd give her a message from him, but that morning Mia received neither.

After work, she headed to her own place since she hadn't heard a word from Morris the entire day. She took a chance on texting him before going to sleep, saying, ***I missed u 2day, gn baby***. All she got back was, ***missed u 2, gn***. *He did at least say that*, she thought before calling it a night, but when it happened again the next day, Mia figured they were now a done deal. She decided she would let him make the next move to call or text first because she wasn't in the business of begging. As fine and well put together as she was, Morris was the lucky one, not her, so she decided to go cold turkey and wait on him to reach out to her.

"Fuck! Men are all the fucking same!" she spat before climbing into her empty bed. She hadn't heard from Morris, so she hoped the next day would be different, but sadly, it wasn't. Again, she hadn't heard a word. "Fuck him too!" she mumbled before falling asleep alone for the second night.

The next morning, she woke up to her doorbell ringing insanely. She focused and wished her roommate was still there to answer the door because she didn't want to move. She scrambled for her robe and made her way to the door. When she opened it, it was Morris. "Good morning, baby, and I'm sorry," he said, reaching out for her hand.

"Morris, it's eight o'clock in the morning," she said and yawned.

"I am aware of that, and I was a jerk. Please forgive me. Our issues," he paused. "My issues," he corrected himself. "Should be shared, and I want to talk about it. No more secrets, Mia. We can discuss our sexual preferences, but for now I have to make a trip to Cali for a day. I've arranged for that car outside to take you to get the most exquisite pampering of your life. Grab your purse and phone and go."

"Baby, I need to get dressed and brush my teeth."

"Brush your teeth, grab a trench coat and don't bother getting dressed. You'll have something to wear by the end of the day," he said and gave her a kiss on the forehead. "I have to catch my flight. I love you, Mia, and I will see you tomorrow. Whatever you want or need, just don't hesitate. These guys," he gave a point to two uniformed men, "will take care of you. Enjoy your day, baby." He gave her another quick kiss and then headed down the steps. Mia had to breathe. It was like a fairytale, and she hated that she wanted more. Morris was the ideal man, but when it came to sex, the only thing she held on to was the first night they shared. If he couldn't deliver that, she wasn't sure if she could stay.

Chapter Thirteen

Reynard

When Rey pulled into the driveway of Lisa's house, there was a silver car parked with Georgia license plates. He wondered who was visiting because Lisa had said nothing about anyone coming to town, and he wondered why he hadn't alerted with a text or a call. It had been three weeks since Lisa's surgery, and it was still too soon for him to return to work. The healing process was very difficult. Though Lisa was doing the right things as the doctor ordered, the first week he had an infection and spent a night in the hospital. He was better now and on the road to a successful recovery, but still in a lot of pain.

Lisa constantly reminded Rey how much he hated dilating his new vagina every day, three times a day. Rey felt awful that Lisa was going through such an ordeal, but he was still anxious to fuck. Rey convinced himself to be content with head, but he couldn't wait to feel Lisa's insides to see if it felt like a real woman's pussy. He was pissed when he heard it would be more than three months before he could fuck Lisa. He was horny as fuck, stressed about his break up and still trying to get over NeNe, so the last thing he wanted was a house guest to be an added problem in life.

He walked in, and Lisa was on the sofa with a blanket and the remote relaxing like he should have been. Reassignment surgery was not a walk in the park, and Rey felt bad for Lisa all the time because he had gone through so much to be what he thought he should have been born with from the very beginning. Two months of rest was what the doctor ordered, and Rey made sure Lisa did nothing to set his healing process back. He did everything in his power to make sure Lisa's recovery was stress and physical free. He even cooked and did all the shopping. Every morning he gave Lisa the same speech before leaving. He'd say, *"If you need anything, call me or call the gym. Don't lift anything in this house other than the remote, a fork to eat with or a glass of something to drink. Don't even think about going anywhere, and other than the bathroom, don't move around too much," he'd order.*

"Okay, Reynard, damn. You just told me the same shit yesterday. I didn't forget," Lisa would pout.

"I know, baby. I just want you to be okay."

"I know," Lisa would smile. No matter what surgery he had, he'd pull his make-up bag from his purse and make up his face. "Just because I'm a recovering patient doesn't mean I have to look like one, hunty!" he told Reynard when he asked why he was putting on make-up every day to go nowhere.

"Hey," Rey said, and Lisa looked up from the television.

"Hey, baby, you're home," Lisa said with excitement and a bright smile plastered over his face.

"Whose car is that outside, babe?" Rey immediately inquired.

"My cousin, Joslyn. She drove all the way up here to help me out while I recover."

"Baby, I'm helping you. I'm taking care of you. You didn't have to bring a relative from out of town to look after you. Lisa, I've been taking care of you," he said as he approached the sofa. He leaned in to kiss him.

"I know, Rey, and you have been awesome, but Joslyn insisted. She was having a little man trouble and needed a break, so—," he whispered, but then he was cut off.

"And here I is," Joslyn chimed in. She had a southern, yet proper speech.

Rey turned to see who the stranger was, and his mouth almost fell wide the fuck open because she was drop dead gorgeous. She stood in the doorway of the guest bedroom looking like she had just stepped out of a fashion magazine. Her hair, make-up and overall appearance were sexy as fuck, and he quickly turned back to Lisa. "Baby, seriously … was I not doing a good job taking care of you? Do we really need someone else here?"

"Yes, you were doing an excellent job, baby, and I appreciate everything, but Joss volunteered."

She made her way over and extended her hand. Rey exchanged a gentle handshake with her. "I'm Joss, and it's a pleasure, Rey. I've heard so much about you."

"Well, I've heard nothing about you," he blurted, being honest.

"No worries, we'll get to know each other soon enough," she said and turned to walk away. She headed towards the kitchen. Rey got a good look at her swollen ass and round hips and prayed his dick wouldn't grow hard right then and there. She wore a body hugging dress that hit her ankles but left nothing to the imagination. S*urgery could never give Lisa a body like that*, Rey thought to himself and knew she had to go or it would definitely be some fucking trouble.

"I hope you're hungry, Rey, because I've made my famous five-cheese Lasagna," she sang.

Rey looked at Lisa. "Are you serious, babe?" he spoke between clenched teeth.

"What, she loves to cook," Lisa whispered.

"How long is she staying?" he asked in a low tone, trying to keep their conversation private.

"I don't know," Lisa whispered back.

"Baby, the last thing we need is a houseguest. A week tops, and she needs to head back to the peach state."

"Baby, damn! This is my house you know, and she is my family," Lisa defended.

Rey changed his tone because he was right. That was his house, not his, so who was he to decide how long a guest could stay. "You're right. Lisa. I'm sorry. I'm going to shower real quick."

"Okay, I'll wait for you to eat."

"No, no, no, no, go ahead if you're ready," Rey insisted.

"No, I'm good. I'll wait for you," Lisa said.

"Okay, babe, I won't be long," he said and gave him another peck before he headed to the master. He tried to keep his eyes off of Joss, but she was bending over taking the Lasagna out of the stove, so he stole a peep at her round ass before he disappeared into the bedroom. Once he was in the shower, he thought of NeNe and then of how sexy Joss' ass was. *Slow your roll, playboy. You don't need no extra drama on your damn plate*, he told himself. After he was clean as a whistle, he got out, moisturized his skin and threw on some long shorts and a tank. He put on a fresh pair of socks and slid his feet into the Ralph Lauren slippers that Lisa had gotten him because he prohibited shoes in his house.

He walked out of the room, and Lisa and Joss were chatting with the television on mute. They both had a glass of red and after the day Rey had, he went for the Crown and made himself one on the rocks. He wanted to snuggle on the couch with Lisa, but he didn't want to be rude to company. He took a seat at the counter on one of the barstools so he wouldn't interrupt their girl chatter.

"Bae, come sit with me on the couch. I haven't seen you all day," Lisa said, patting the cushion.

"Naw, I'm good. I don't want to impose on you and your cuzzo's convo," he told her.

"Nonsense, Rey. Come on over and join us. We were about to fix plates anyway," she said and stood. "Do you want your salad in a bowl or on the same plate? I don't have a dishwasher at home, so mostly all of my food goes on the same plate," she laughed.

"No, I'm good, Joss. I can fix me and Lisa's plates. I don't need you to fix them," Rey refuted.

"Can you believe him?" Joss asked, looking at Lisa. "Can you tell this man how we do it," Joss said.

"Rey, the women in my family cook and serve, don't act like you don't know. Before my surgery, have you ever cooked or fixed a plate?"

Rey paused. "Ummm, I guess no," he said, shaking his head from side to side.

"Thank you, so relax and let Joss take care of it. I don't mind," Joss smiled. Rey took a gulp of his drink and wondered why he felt uneasy. Was it because Joss was so damn attractive, or was it because his dick needed to be inside some pussy? He'd thought of just hooking up with a chick at the gym, but he didn't want that drama because he already knew women couldn't keep their legs or damn mouths closed, so he declined on that. Plus, he didn't want any more scandal at work. If half the women he fucked brought that shit to Rayshon, he'd be out of a good job. He was the GM for crying out loud, making good money to do practically nothing. His job was a walk in the park, so he didn't want shit to jeopardize that. Rayshon was the best boss he had ever had, and he didn't want to disappoint him, so hook-ups with members were no longer an option.

"Fine," he agreed and finished his drink. Before the plates were on the dining table, he helped slow moving Lisa over to sit and then refilled his glass. They sat and when Joss reached for their hands to bless the food, Rey looked at Lisa. They never prayed before digging in. Lisa gave him a nod, and he took Joss' soft hand. It felt like a woman's hand, not like Lisa's. Lisa's hands weren't rough, but they were not petite like a woman's. Rey felt some kind of way but quickly reminded himself that he loved Lisa. He gave up everything for Lisa, so it was no turning back, and he had to be faithful for once in his adult life.

Joss prayed and gave Rey's hand a squeeze before she let go. Rey found that odd, but he didn't address it. They ate, and he had to admit it was damn good. He volunteered to clean the kitchen while Lisa went back to the sofa. He served them a refill and then went to clean and put away the leftovers. He half listened to them talk about reality shows and how Joss had done hair for a couple of the ladies from *The Real House Wives of Atlanta* a time or two. She bragged about her skills, and Lisa insisted she hook his hair up before going back to Atlanta because he knew with his healing time, he couldn't visit Legacy to get his weave redone.

"Legacy?" Rey asked. "Did you say Legacy?"

"Yes, why?" Lisa asked. "Do you know a stylist name Legacy?"

"Does she work at Sassy Styles?"

"Yes, and how the fuck do you know that?"

Rey tossed the oven mitt onto the counter. "Now it all makes fucking sense. Did you mention me at all to her?"

"Well yeah, we talked."

"What did you tell her?" he demanded. His voice was stern, and he could see that it made Lisa uncomfortable by the way he adjusted the covers he was under.

"Nothing personal, why?" Lisa's neck rolled.

"Legacy is one of Anika's best friends. How on earth out of all the salons in the city of Chicago did you end up there?" he yelled.

"Oh, no! Not in here, not now, not ever, Reynard!" Lisa retorted.

"Baby, I'm sorry for yelling, but please tell me how on earth did you end up in Legacy's chair?"

"There were cards on the advertisement table at the gym, Rey. Why does it fucking matter? I didn't lie," Lisa defended.

Rey calmed down and changed his tone. He knew Lisa was doing the norm, something all women did, which was run off at the fucking mouth. “You’re right, baby, and I’m sorry. You know Anika is sick, and I just didn’t want her to find out about us the way she did. She threw me out, so that means Legacy said something. Either way, no worries, babe, things went down as they should have.”

“I’m not worried, and I don’t care if she was friends with yo’ ex. The bottom line is that you’re here, and I don’t give a fuck about all that other shit. Joss is here, and she’ll make sure I stay looking fabulous,” Lisa said, twisting his neck. Rey was glad that Lisa didn’t react like a real woman and want to go give Legacy a beat down for running her mouth. Lisa saw it as a good thing because it opened the door for them to be together, so Rey buried that conversation, but he would tell Legacy’s ass a thing or two the next time he saw her fat ass.

Chapter Fourteen

LaTanya

"Hey, Chantel, come on back," she told her last client. She had been busier than ever, and her days seemed to be longer since she was pregnant, plus she felt more sluggish and tired throughout her day. "Lord, God give me strength," she mumbled as she followed her client back to the shampoo bowl. All her stylists had gone and since she was now moving in slow motion, she knew she had to lighten her load of clients because she could no longer maintain.

"How are you doing, Tanya? You look worn out," Chantel said.

"I am struggling, girl. I am tired all the time now and can't seem to get enough rest."

Chantel sat, and Tanya draped her neck with a towel before putting a smock over her clothes. "Are you taking your vitamins?" Chantel asked.

"I am, but I'm so exhausted. It's not only morning sickness, it's afternoon and evening too. I can't keep nothing down."

"Chile, soon it will pass," she encouraged.

"I hope so," Tanya said as she shampooed her client's head. She shifted from leg to leg because she felt an annoying cramp. "Oh, Lord, please," she said out loud.

"Are you okay?"

"I'm feeling a little discomfort, but I'm sure it's nothing. I had a long day. Still launching my hair products and doing hair, girl. I'm still trying to be superwoman before—" She paused because a cramp hit her hard. "Ahhh, ahhh," she grunted and bent over the sink. She reached to turn off the water so she wouldn't get water all over her client and the floor.

Chantel sat up. "Tanya, are you okay?"

"I don't know. I, I, ahhh, oh my God, Chantel! This hurts, I need to use the bathroom," she expressed, and Chantel stood to assist. Chantel grabbed a towel and wrapped it around her wet hair. Tanya turned to head towards the bathroom.

"Oh shit, Tanya, we need to call 911," she said in a panic.

"No, I just have to go to the bathroom."

"Tanya, your pants is full of blood," she told her, and Tanya instantly panicked.

"No, no, no, it can't be," she cried and reached down to feel her soiled crotch. "Dial 911, please and get my phone, I have to call Kenny," she shrieked.

Chantel dug in her purse while she hurried to Tanya's station to get her phone. She rushed back to Tanya's side, and Tanya could hear her explaining the emergency. By then Tanya was on the floor in unbearable pain, and her hands shook as she called Kenny. "I don't' know what is going on, but there is something wrong. I'm going to the hospital by ambulance, I will call you when I'm there," she said to Kenny's voicemail. Within minutes, the paramedics were there, and she was hauled off to the hospital. She heard her phone going off back to back, but there was no way they would let her answer it. By the time she made it to the hospital, she had miscarried, and she was devastated.

She sobbed uncontrollably when the doctors explained that there was nothing they could have done to save her baby. She laid there and then finally called Kenny back, and he was at her side within a half hour.

"Oh, my God, Tanya! Are you okay? What happened?" he cried. He had a look on his face that Tanya had never seen before. A look of love and sincerity, and she felt that the baby was the only thing she had that could bring him back to her.

"I'm fine, Kenny, and I'm okay. We're okay. The baby and I are fine. I had some bleeding and discomfort and panicked, but it's all good. I just have to be on bed rest. I can't go back to work until the doctor says so, so I am going to need you to help me," she lied to his face. She could not bring herself to tell him that there was no baby. They had been getting along so well, and Kenny was coming around and spending time with her. She didn't want to give that up, and she was nowhere near ready to tell him she had lost the baby. That was the only way she could win him back.

Since Kenny had demanded a DNA test, she was terrified because it was a big chance the baby wasn't his, but her plans were just to get him back into her good graces and away from Legacy's fat ass. Hell, she was far more beautiful, way more successful and was on the rise, how could he want Legacy over her?

"Anything you need, Tanya, anything. I'll be here for you and this baby, so don't worry."

"What about Legacy?"

"Don't worry about Legacy. She knows all too well about bed rest. She's been through it, so she knows how I am. I didn't leave her in the cold, so why would I do that to you?"

She smiled. "Thank you, Kenny, because I was worried. You know I was worried. I have no one to call on."

"You got me, and I know you may hate the idea, but Legacy will help out too. She doesn't hate you," he said.

"No, no, no, and hell to the no! She and I can't be in the same room. I need a stress-free environment for your baby, and I can't deal with Legacy," she disputed.

"I got you. I understand. Don't worry," he said and reached to rub her stomach. She flinched. "What's wrong?"

"I don't want you to touch my stomach, Kenny. That's weird, I'm not comfortable with that."

"Wow, that's odd, but okay. I don't want you feeling any type of way because of me. I just want a healthy son," he expressed.

She smiled. "You want a baby boy?"

He hesitated. "Yes," he admitted. "It would be nice to have a son. I have two beautiful daughters, but I must admit that I hope it's a boy."

"I hope so too," she said. She smiled at him, and he rested his head on her stomach. She didn't know if it was a boy or girl, all she knew is the DNC had cleaned out all traces of a fetus from her uterus. She knew she was wrong and wondered how she would come clean, but that night she just let him rest his head on her tummy and the tears stream from her eyes. Although she played the game unfairly to get him, she loved him and knew he was the best man for her. Were her eyes on another prize? Fuck yes. She was fucking around with a married man that she knew she'd never have, but he was brilliant and could help her sky rocket her career.

Kenny was just her type. She'd never admit it to him, but she loved a blue-collared man that came home with dirty hands and a soiled uniform. She loved how masculine and strong Kenny was, and he did fuck her right. Yes, she played him occasionally, but that was her way of keeping him in check to let him know she was in charge, but somehow it backfired. When he caught her kissing Anthony, she thought she could talk her way out of it, but instead he left and ran right back to fat ass Legacy.

Tanya hated her ass because she always knew in the back of her mind that Kenny had never gotten over her. As unattractive as Tanya thought she was, Legacy had the power to take Kenny back. A week after he was gone, she learned she was pregnant but had contemplated on an abortion because she didn't know which one had knocked her up, but then she figured it would be a way to get her man back since Anthony's married ass wasn't going to leave his wife.

"So, when can you go home?" Kenny asked, interrupting her thoughts.

"Tomorrow I assume. Will you be able to come back and take me? I was brought here by ambulance, and my car is still at my shop."

"Let me know the exact time, and I'll figure something out."

"Okay. Thank you, Kenny. I don't want to go through this pregnancy alone."

"You won't. I already told you before tonight that I'm here. Where have I been the past couple of weeks before going home?"

"With me."

"Exactly. I'm all in, Tanya. I just hope you're telling me the truth. You said I'm the only one you've fucked with, and I believe you. Just please be honest. If this baby isn't mine and I'm going through all of this with you and breaking Legacy's heart, I will never be able to forgive you."

"Kenny, this baby is yours. You are the only one I've been with since you and I got together. There is no doubt in my mind, and I'm telling you the honest to God truth," she lied big time. There was no more baby and even if there were, she still couldn't guarantee that Kenny was the father. She didn't have long to figure out what to do next, but for now she'd stick to her story and hope to win him back.

Chapter Fifteen

Anika

Anika looked at the clock and then readjusted the covers. It was close to eleven o'clock at night, and Jaxson still hadn't made it to her place. She didn't want to call him or text, so she closed her eyes and tried to get some sleep. She had been the one to allow him to go to the hospital to be with his ex, so if he and Michelle were fucking at that very moment, she'd have herself to blame. She trusted Jaxson and believed him when he said he was over and done with Michelle and that he loved her, but she had a sinking feeling he wasn't being totally honest.

Moments like this sometimes drew people closer together, but she hoped Jaxson was who he claimed to be because she agreed to trust him and not let her past relationship with Rey ruin it for them. Jaxson promised that he'd leave her before he would ever break her heart, and she believed him, so she allowed herself to drift off to sleep.

"Baby," she heard, and her eyes fluttered. She looked up to see him and then glanced at the clock. It was after midnight, so she hadn't been sleeping that long.

"You're home, babe," she smiled.

He leaned in to kiss her. "Yes, I'm home, baby. I'm sorry it's so late," he apologized and kissed her again.

"It's okay. How is Michelle's mom?"

"Not good. Michelle took her home because there is nothing else that can be done. She feels it's best that her mom go home and rest until she passes."

"Wow, that's sad. I'm so sorry. I don't know how close you are to Michelle's mom, so are you okay?"

"Yes, I'm okay. I care for Norma just as much as I care for my own mom, and I hate to see Michelle and her family go through something like this. Norma has been sick a long time, so we knew this day would soon come."

"Does Michelle have any siblings?"

"Yeah, a sister and an older brother. Her brother lives out in D.C., but he should be home tomorrow."

"Good, then maybe she won't depend on you so much?"

"Baby, come on, don't be that way. I'm not only there for Michelle. I am there for me as well. Norma was an amazing woman and a great mother-in-law, so don't think it's about Michelle. Please get those thoughts out of your head," he said and caressed her face. "I promise you there is nothing there between Michelle and me. I love you, NeNe, and you have nothing to be afraid of. I'd never break your heart," he smiled at her.

"You promise?" she pleaded. She hated sounding so needy, but she needed to be sure he was sincere.

"Yes, baby, I promise. Now let me shower, and I'll climb into this bed and show you just how much I love you," he said and leaned in for another kiss. She grabbed the back of his head and pulled him closer. She didn't want him to leave her side.

"Nah, baby, take me right now," she moaned. He kissed her neck and made his way down to her breasts. Her nipples were flat, but after he massaged and licked them, they transformed into pebbles, and Jaxson wasted no time pleasing them. He went from left to right, sucking, licking and nibbling, and NeNe expressed her appreciation with loud moans and naughty words. When he headed south, she didn't stop him. She spread her legs wide and let his tongue and fingers bring her to her first orgasm.

She whined her hips and met his tongue as she rose from the bed. It felt so good to cum, and she wanted another one. "No, baby, don't stop. Make me cum again, give me another one," she moaned while gripping the sheets. It was an intense feeling for her to allow him to continue to suck and lick, but in the past she'd had back-to-back orgasms if she suffered through the sensitive moments that occurred right after the first one. She let her ass fall back to the mattress and released the grip she had on the sheets and grabbed the back of Jaxson's head. She wanted another explosive nut, so she made sure his tongue stayed right on her bulb and within seconds, she got it.

That time she came harder than the first time, and the feeling was so intense that it pained her a little, but it was one of the best climaxes she'd had in a long time. "Now you," she panted, trying to catch her breath.

Jaxson stood and removed his clothes because she hadn't given him a chance to undress. With his tool erect, he moved back over to the bed and stood on the side and told her to get on all fours. Once she was in position, he stroked his shaft and rubbed his head over her lips. The heat that came from his body warmed her lips, and she let the tip of her tongue slip past her lips.

"Yes, baby, yessssssssssss," he hissed. "Stick that tongue out for me," he ordered, and she obeyed. He tapped his head on her tongue and then pushed his way into her mouth. He grabbed the sides of her head with his strong hands and worked his pelvis, pushing his pole in and out of her mouth. NeNe moaned as her lover shoved his dick deep into her mouth, hitting the back of her throat.

"Yes, baby, take this dick, suck it, suck this dick," he growled. "You gon' make me shoot all this down your throat," he grunted. He was a great lover and very passionate in bed, but tonight he was in fuck mode, and NeNe liked it. She loved the way he talked to her and the way he held her face as she pleased him. Nene pulled back, flipped over on her back and let her head drop over the side of the bed. He leaned into the bed and slid his dick back into her mouth. She gagged, but took each one of his strokes like a porn star. Saliva ran down the sides of her jaws while he stroked her mouth until he exploded. She thought he would cum in her mouth, but he pulled out and laced her tits and stomach with his hot lava. He jerked and moaned until it was all out, and she giggled.

"Damn, NeNe, that was some wicked ass head. That shit felt better than ever," he panted.

"Did you like that, baby?" she said, rubbing his nut into her skin.

"Like it? Baby, I loved that shit," he said and then flopped down on the bed. "Come take a shower with me," he said.

She turned on her side and rested her head on her propped up elbow and hand. "Start the water. I need a glass of water," she said. He stood and headed for the bathroom, and she got up and went to the kitchen. She downed a bottle of water and then went to join Jaxson in the shower. On her way she heard his phone, and then she looked at the clock. It was close to one. She tried to resist, but she went into his pocket and pulled out his phone. The screen read *Micky*, and she guessed that was short for Michelle. She held the phone and looked at it until it stopped ringing. She put the phone back into his pocket and went to join him in the bathroom and didn't mention his missed call. "What took you so long?" he asked when she stepped in.

"That wasn't long," she defended.

"It felt like an eternity," he joked and pulled her close. The hot water cascaded down their skin, and they played around with the body gel lathering each other's skin. After a second rinse, Jaxson sat on the shower bench, and NeNe straddled him. He licked her breasts and nipples before he spread her ass cheeks, and she slid down onto his erection. She wrapped her legs around his waist and slid back and forth. She couldn't remember Rey ever feeling that damn good inside of her body. Jaxson's long and thick dick glided in and out of her nectar so smoothly that she never wanted to stop. She wrapped her arms around his neck and pushed her tongue inside of his mouth, and his kiss intensified the energy between them. She felt her center quicken. "Ahhh fuck, baby, fuck. I'm cumming again. It's so good, it's soooo, ahhhh!" she screamed. Her thighs trembled, and she rode him harder to let it all out. She held on to his neck tighter and then sucked his tongue. He felt amazing and even though she had cum three times, she still wanted more of him. She squatted and grabbed his shaft. She stroked him in her fist and sucked his head as hard as she could clench her jaws.

"Shit baby, shit, NeNe," the guttural sounds came from deep inside his throat. "No, baby. No, please stop, I want more of your wet pussy," Jaxson hissed. He pulled his dick away from her grasp, and then she stood. The water was getting cool, but neither of them said a word about getting out. "Bend that ass over," Jaxson ordered, stroking his rock hard dick in his palm. The head was shining, and his veins were imprinted all around his rod, and NeNe's pussy throbbed for him. She bent over and rested her hands on the bench. He grabbed a hold of her hips and instead of using his hands to guide himself in, he let the head of his dick find its own way inside of her.

"Ahhhh, yasssssss!" she squealed. "Do me, baby, do me right. I love the way your dick feels inside of me, baby, yassssss," she continued. He hit her with hard strokes and mixed in some long deep ones. He'd pull completely out and dip back in, and the only thing NeNe could do is moan and call out his name.

Whap, whap, whap, were the sounds of him slapping her ass as he fucked her to ecstasy. He grabbed her waist tightly and rolled deep inside of her, and NeNe could feel his dick up in her stomach. He was pressing so deep on her cervix, it hurt, but she took it.

"Yea, baby, yes, yea. I have to go deep, baby, because I'm about to nut right now!" he groaned and gripped her skin tighter. He pumped hard and fast and the sounds he made, made NeNe smile. She had given her man all of her, and she felt damn good.

He slid out, and she stood and turned to him. She wrapped her arms around his neck, and he wrapped his arms around her waist, and they held each other tight.

"I love you, baby," she whispered.

"And I love you too, NeNe," he whispered back.

"Can we go to sleep now?"

"Hell yes!"

They got out, dried their skin and got into bed naked. Now that it was close to 2:00 a.m., they were out within moments.

The next morning before he moved out of her bed, he slid in from the back while they both rested on their sides. NeNe was sore and worn out, but she let him beat the pussy and twerk her nipples as long as he liked until he released inside of her again. He left her in bed and went to shower. She dragged herself to the kitchen to get breakfast going and when Jaxson came out in a towel, she wanted to lick the specks of water from his chest.

He had his phone in his hand, and the look on his face was sadness. "Baby, what's wrong?" NeNe inquired.

"Michelle called me ten times last night. She text saying that her mother passed away."

NeNe's mouth fell open. She felt horrible that she hadn't alerted him that his phone rang. "Oh my God, JT, I'm so sorry," she said and hurried to his side. She put her arms around him, and he put an arm around her.

"It's okay, baby, but I must call her. I know she's a wreck."

NeNe didn't want her man running to his ex's side, but she nodded like a good girlfriend and watched her man head off into the other room to call his soon to be ex-wife.

Fuck!

Chapter Sixteen

Legend

He had the entire evening planned for him and Jackie. It was their seventh anniversary, and he wanted to surprise her with a weekend getaway. Legacy had agreed to stay at his house and watch the girls since his house was larger than her condo, and he couldn't wait to show up at her office to take her away for their romantic weekend. He had already packed her toiletries and his favorite fragrance. Legacy helped him pick out some nice lingerie and new matching panty and bra sets because that weekend he didn't want to see her in any clothes. All he wanted to do was order in, sip champagne and make love to his wife.

He pulled up to her office building and pulled out his tablet to check on his reservations for Grand Geneva Resort & Spa in Lake Geneva, Wisconsin. It would be a little less than a two-hour drive, so he wanted to make sure everything was in order. After he confirmed, he put his tablet back into the arm rest of his SUV and then popped a mint into his mouth. He got out and ran a hand down his Ralph Lauren button down and jeans and adjusted his Biltmore/Belfry Harley–Fedora. He had on a pair of Alexander McQueen low top boots, and the fragrance of John Varvatos dripped from his skin. So, not only did he look good, he smelled divine. Legend caught a glimpse of himself in the reflection of his shiny black Escalade and smiled. He wasn't as young as the day they had met, but he was still sexy and could still turn heads.

He headed towards the building, and all eyes were on him as he walked through the main floor to get to the elevators. When he landed on her floor, he expected to see her receptionist, Aubrey, at her desk, but she wasn't there. It looked as if her computer was off and that she had already gone for the day. Legend proceeded and when he reached for the doorknob, he paused because he heard the sound of his wife giggling, a sound he enjoyed. He wondered what tickled her, so he turned the door handle, but it was locked. He stood still for a moment and listened in before he tapped because what was a giggle were now soft moans and sounds of pleasure. Legend rested his palms on the door and then laid his ear on the wood to listen closer, and he heard the sounds of a man groaning and skin slapping. Anger took over his body, and he didn't know what to do at the moment. He couldn't even think straight, all he could see was red. Before he could stop himself, he took two steps back and then kicked in the door. The loud bang jolted his wife and her lover, and they both had a sheer look of panic on their faces.

"Legend!" Jackie cried, and her lover pulled out of her and took a couple steps back. Jackie moved fast as lighting to her clothes that were scattered around her office. With each item she grabbed, she scrambled to get dressed.

Her lover stood frozen with a hard dick extended from his body. He held up his hands. "Look, man, I'm sorry," he said nervously, like he was afraid to go for his clothes.

"Don't say a motherfucking word to me!" he barked at the stranger.

"Legend, baby, please," Jackie cried with shaky hands. She could barely button the buttons on her blouse.

"Please what, huh?" he blasted. He walked up to her and grabbed her face with one hand, and it took every muscle in his body to keep from knocking her ass to the floor, but he squeezed the fuck out of her face. "You are a stupid ass whore. You'd do this to me, to us, to our family? You have stood your lying whore ass in my face and promised me that there was no one else, that I was imagining things, but here you are up here in your fucking office fucking this nigga like a nasty ass ho!" he spat in her face.

"I'm sorry," she tried to speak, but he held her face so tight her words weren't clear.

He pushed her face when he released her from his grasp. "You are sorry!" he spat. He saw her lover finally move towards his clothes. "No, don't mind me, man. I'm leaving, so you two can pick up where you left off. I'll go so you can bend this whore back over her desk and fuck her nasty ass pussy," he spat with venom. He pulled off his ring and threw it across the room. "We're fucking done. Happy anniversary!" he bellowed and then turned to walk away.

She ran after him. "Legend, baby, Legend, wait!" she called out, but he kept going. He stopped at the elevators and hit the call button and then she caught up to him. She reached for him, but he backed away.

"Don't fucking touch me, Jacqueline!"

"Please wait, let's talk. I'm so sorry, baby. I know what I did was fucked up, but this was the first time, I swear it," she cried. Her face was drenched with tears, but he didn't give not one fuck.

He looked at her like she was a bitch on the streets. "If you don't get your lying ass out of my face I'm going to motherfucking jail today because as God as my witness, I will knock your motherfucking head off your shoulders!" he roared and then the elevator doors opened. "*Move*!" he yelled.

Defeated, she let him pass. He got on the elevator and looked at his wife of seventeen years with her clothes hanging off her body looking like a mess. The image of her bent over her desk with some man's dick moving in and out of her would forever be etched in his brain. He wished he had called first. He wished he'd given her the heads up before going up to her office.

He hit the alarm on his SUV and climbed into the driver's seat. The image played in his mind, and then he remembered the flowers he had sent her were right on the desk that she was bent over on. His eyes burned with tears, and he was hurt. How could she? He had plenty of opportunities to fuck around with other women, but he never gave another woman the time of day in all the years he had been with Jackie. He had never strayed. Never once did he ever cheat on her, and he was sitting in his vehicle broken hearted and angry as fuck. He wanted to march back up to her office and tear shit up. He wanted to beat the fuck out of her lover, but what good would that do? That wouldn't change that his wife fucked him. It wouldn't make any difference. All that would do is get his ass locked up.

Legend pushed the button to start his engine and then put the car in reverse. He then thought of her bag in the back, so he put the car back into park and got out and retrieved her bag. He grabbed it and tossed it onto the ground near her driver's side door. He was sure she'd recognize the bag. He hopped back into his vehicle and was about to head home, but he took a detour. He didn't want to see his daughter's right then because he was too upset and didn't want the words, "Your mother is a cheating whore," to rain from his lips if they asked what was wrong. He headed to Jay's, a spot a friend of his owned.

As soon as he got on the Dan Ryan, Jackie called his phone repeatedly. She'd text and then call, and then text again, begging him to take her call. ***Where r u, we need 2 tlk,*** she text.

He continued on his route not bothering to answer. By the time he arrived at his destination, she had called over a dozen times. He was about to open his door to get out, but she called one more time, and that time he answered. "What in the fuck do you want, Jackie? Why do you keep calling my got'damn phone!" he blasted.

"Legend, please. I made a mistake, honey. I fucked up royally, and I am so sorry. I need to talk to you. I need you!" she cried.

"Are you fucking crazy, Jacqueline? Please tell me, are you touched in the motherfucking head? I just busted open the motherfucking door to a man pounding the fuck out of my wife while she was bent over a motherfucking desk in her office like some two-dollar whore, so what do you have to say?"

"I'm sorry, Legend. Please, baby, I'm begging you to just come home so we can talk."

"Home! Bitch, you better not think about carrying your lying ass home. I left your bag by your car door, find yourself somewhere else to lay yo' head tonight!"

"No, no, no, Legend. You can't throw me out. What will you tell the kids?"

"The fucking truth! Their momma got caught in her office ass naked with some nigga fucking her from the back!" he growled. He was so mad, he could spit in her face. His heart ached, and he didn't want to see her or even be in the same room with her.

"Please just come home," she sniffled. He said nothing. "Legend, I'm so fucking sorry. I was wrong, and yes I did a ho'ish thing, and I was wrong honey. Please, I'm begging you."

"No!" he snapped and hung up. His eyes welled, and he was in no shape to go into a bar either. "Fuck!" He punched the steering wheel when his tears rolled down his face. He took his hat off and tossed it on the passenger seat and sat there to get himself together. Legend didn't want to see her or talk to her, but he knew they didn't need to be around their children until they talked and made some decisions. He grabbed his phone and dialed her back.

“Hello,” she answered on the first ring.

“Where are you?”

“In the parking lot at my office,” she said. He could hear in her voice that she was still sobbing.

“I’m on my way to pick you up. Don’t leave!” he ordered and ended the call. They were going on their trip as planned, but he wanted to discuss his divorce and break the news to her that he was taking the kids. No way was she leaving with a dime his money and after the scene he witnessed earlier, he would not only ask for child support, but he was also asking for alimony. When men fuck up, women are quick to bring a man to his knees and take everything. If he had been caught in his office with some bitch bent over his desk, she’d do the same, so that’s exactly what he planned to do to her. “Trifling bitch,” he mumbled and then started his engine.

Chapter Seventeen

Kenny

Kenny sat in his car talking to Legacy on the phone before going into Tanya's house. Legacy was at her brother's for the weekend, and he told her he was going to hang out for a little while with the fellas and then come by there. Legend's house was enormous, and there was a guestroom equipped with a private bathroom, so that was where he and the kids would spend their weekend. He loved his brother-in-law's house because Legend had a man cave that Kenny knew he'd someday have, and that is where he'd be that weekend while Legacy took care of all the girls. He hung up with Legacy after promising her that he wouldn't be out too late. He turned off his engine and got out and walked up Tanya's walkway. She had been bugging him for some Shrimp Egg Fu-Yong, and he had promised he'd stop by with some after work.

He remembered Legacy's craving for banana splits, and she only wanted hers from Original Rainbow Cone on 92nd and Western. That summer when she was pregnant with Kierra, they'd go every other day. He had fun with Legacy during her first pregnancy, but with Kennedy she had to go on bed rest, and he wondered why the same thing had to happen to Tanya. He opened the door with the key she had given back to him the night they got together to talk things out about the baby. They had been civil since then, the only time there was turbulence is when she and Legacy were in the same room. They couldn't stand each other.

Legacy promised Tanya that she knew that baby wasn't Kenny's, and Tanya swore she'd slap the shit out of Legacy once the results were in. He tried to keep the peace, but no baby on earth would make them two like each other ever again. If Legacy had all the facts, he was sure she wouldn't want to see his ass ever again.

"It's me, Tanya," Kenny yelled out when he walked in. Normally, Tanya would be upstairs in bed with the remote and a box of tissue. Everything made her emotional, and she was crying all the time, especially at baby commercials.

"You know where I am," she yelled back. "You betta have my damn food, Kenny. If not, don't even bring yo' ass up these damn stairs," she continued to yell.

"Tanya, calm the fuck down. I got yo' food. You'd think I'd come here empty handed to hear yo' ass fuss and cuss?" Kenny headed to the kitchen, washed his hands and opened the cartons and fixed her a plate. "Do you need something to drink?" he yelled out. He didn't want to have to run up and down the stairs for shit.

"Naw, I'm good," she yelled back. He went up to the bedroom where she was sitting up in bed with a tray across her thighs.

"What's all this?" he asked, looking around. Her room looked like a mini kitchen.

"A few girls from my salon came by today with all these goodies." There was a table set up against the wall near the bed with all kinds of snacks on it. On the night stand sat what looked like an oversized lunch box, but Kenny soon learned it was a mini ice chest. "Since I'll be laid up for a while, they thought this would make my life easier to keep me from going up and down the stairs so much."

"That was thoughtful," he said and put her plate on the tray in front of her.

"It was," she said and then picked up the fork. "We about to get our grub on ain't we, lil man?" she said, rubbing her stomach. She bowed her head a second and then dug in.

"How are you feeling today? Are you keeping track of the baby's movements?"

"Yes, Kenny, I am, damn. Why do you ask me that shit every day?"

"Because I want to make sure, got'dammit! When do we go back to the doctor? It's been two weeks. I was sure she'd want to see you by now. When Legacy was on bed rest, we had to go in once a week."

"I went to the doctor yesterday, Kenny."

"You did? Why didn't you tell me?" he asked.

"Because it was last minute. The nurse called and said they had a cancellation and could get me in. You were at work, so one of my stylists took me. No biggie."

"No biggie? I would have left work, Tanya. I told you I want to go to every appointment. I want to hear everything the doctor says in case I have questions about the health of my child."

"Kenny, calm the fuck down. It was just a routine check-up. The baby's heart rate was a little low, but nothing to be alarmed about, and she told me to stay on bed rest. She said I can move around and take short walks around the house, but no heavy lifting. We're fine, me and your son is fine, so don't worry your pretty little head."

"Whatever, Tanya. Don't do that shit again. I want to be a part of this, and that means going to the doctor."

She nodded and continued to stuff her face. When she was done, he took her plate downstairs and rinsed it. He went back up and got in bed beside her. She rested her head on his shoulder, and when he reached to touch her tummy, she swatted his hand. "Stop, Kenny, I told you that is weird. I don't want you touching my stomach."

"Why is that weird, LaTanya? I just want to feel my kid move. I have never felt him kick or move."

"And you won't until he's here. That makes me feel uncomfortable, and you know it. I don't need you over here stressing me out," she barked.

"Okay, okay. Damn, Tanya, relax. I just don't see how me touching you makes you feel some type of way. When Legacy was pregnant, I rubbed her belly all the time."

"If you say one more word about you and Legacy's pregnancies, I'm going to scream. I'm so fucking tired of you comparing everything to her, damn. Why can't my pregnancy be my pregnancy? She and I are two damn different individuals and if I have to hear her name one mo'gin, I'm going to scream!"

"Aw'ight, aw'ight, damn woman, calm the fuck down. It's not that serious. All I wanted to do is feel my kid move, but if that makes it weird for you, fine, I won't ask anymore," Kenny sighed. Then he leaned in towards her stomach. "Don't worry, little man, ya' dad loves you. Your momma is the one who's crazy," Kenny joked, and Tanya hit him again.

"What you can do is rub my feet," she smiled.

"Oh, now you want me to cut up my fingers?"

"Whatever, rub my feet," she playfully ordered. Kenny took a seat at the opposite end of the bed and placed a pillow underneath her feet. He massaged her feet, and she laid her head back to relax. "Don't get too comfy, ma'am. I can't stay too long. I promised Legacy I wouldn't be too late."

"Uggghhh, Kenny, damn! Don't say her name again. You are going to send me back to emergency."

"Stop being so dramatic, Tanya. You know her reasons for not liking yo' ass and now that this baby is on the way, there is a lot of tension at home."

"Is there?"

"Yes. I mean, we're cool and civil, but the looks she gives me sometimes. I, I, I just know she's disappointed."

Tanya rested her hands on her belly. "Well, I can't say I'm sorry because I'm not. This baby was conceived when we were together, so she'll just have to deal with it."

"She is, Tanya, damn! Haven't you been listening? She's not mad at the baby or even you for getting pregnant, she's just more disappointed because now that we finally got our shit together, this had to happen. It's like a gut punch to our happily ever after."

"Well, what about my happily ever after? Do you ever stop to think about me? I know you love Legacy and want to be with her and make her your wife, but I'm about to be a single mother and…" she paused and put her head down.

"And what?"

"The man I love and want to be with is marrying someone else."

"Come on, Tanya, cut the crap. You weren't feeling me anymore. Look how you were acting and how you treated me. You became like this ice queen, and you barely wanted me to touch you."

"It was not because I stopped loving you, Kenny. I had so much going on with trying to get my career off the ground. I didn't have time to just be laying on my back so your dick could feel wanted. I needed a cheering squad, but it's like you were mad because I wanted success."

"I'm sorry you felt that way, Tanya. It wasn't about you being my bed maid, it was about balance. I wanted you to shine, hell I still do, but there must be a balance. All the money you call yourself chasing, you put us on the shelf, and I'm not some toy you can put away and pull out when you want to cum. And then there was your colleague, your business partner, Anthony. Let's not forget him."

"As if you weren't still fucking Legacy," she snapped back and gave Kenny a 'nigga, don't play with me' look.

He was quiet, but then he confessed. "You're right, I was. Every time you told me not tonight, or I got to be here or there and couldn't fit me into your schedule, I was with Legacy. I'll admit it. I was wrong, but you made it easy."

"So did she," she returned.

"I can't speak for her. All I can say is she allowed me to do what I did because of her feelings. Sometimes we get caught in our feelings, but whether you believe it or not, she finally turned me down and turned me away. She vowed that she was moving on without me and told me if I came for her, I'd have to come correct. That night I caught you with Anthony, I had come to break things off with you. I cared, Tanya, but I wasn't feeling you anymore, and I knew then that I loved her and wanted to be with her more than you." Her eyes welled. "I'm not saying any of this to hurt your feelings, but I want to be honest."

She sniffled and was quiet for a moment. She grabbed a few tissues from her box and wiped her eyes and nose. "I have a confession too."

"What is it? What do you want to tell me?"

She hesitated before speaking. "I only decided to have this baby because I thought it would bring you back to me."

He stopped rubbing her feet and went to hold her. "I'm sorry you made that decision based on that, but I'm happy you told me. No way would I have agreed for you to abort my kid."

"I know. Just promise me you won't turn your back on us ever."

"I promise," he said, and then his phone alerted him of a text. He read it, and it was Legacy. "Listen, I need to head out. Do you need anything else?"

She wiped her eyes. "No, Kenny, I'm good."

"Well, I'm going to head out. You get some rest. Try to stay off your feet."

"I will."

"Promise," he smiled.

"I promise," she smiled back. He leaned in and gave her a kiss. That time he kissed her lips. She smiled at him, and he left. He got in the car and text Legacy back, ***I'm on my way baby***.

Chapter Eighteen

Rene

Rene walked past her office again, and she still pretended not to notice him. He missed her so much and hated himself for lying to Laurie because he didn't want to work it out. He loved Laurie, and if he had to spend the rest of his life with her, he'd settle for that, but he desired Mia. Since his desires for Mia were so deep, half the shit that Laurie did was like a pain in his ass, and they only thing they had in common was fucking. Laurie had transformed into a super freak and was giving Rene sex when and wherever he wanted it. She had become so wild with him that she'd want to fuck in public places. She'd want to find a closet, an empty room, anywhere to keep his dick from falling into Mia's pussy, but all the fucking in the world didn't stop him from wanting to have Mia. Renee fantasized and dreamed about her when he closed his eyes and imagined he was fucking her almost every time he was with Laurie. He had to find a way to get back in, had to figure out a way to get her back.

He had to make her his lover again. If nothing else, he needed her physically. He had to touch her, fuck her and make her scream. He and Mia may have been off in other areas, but in the bedroom they were in sync with one another. She knew what to say, what to do and how to make him weak, and he needed her back. He had to have her back, or he'd lose his mind.

"What is it, Rene? Why do you keep stalking me?" Mia spoke loud enough for him to hear her from the hall.

"Oh, hey, Mia, I didn't realize you were in," he lied as he walked into her office.

"Really? Who are you trying to kid, Rene? You've walked by like ten times this morning. I can smell your funky ass cologne," she hissed.

"My cologne is one of your favorites, you—," he tried to say.

She cut him off. "Use to be one of my favorites, now it smells like shit. What do you want? I have work to do. I don't want to have to shut my door, but if you don't stop coming by every five fucking minutes, I will." He took a few steps back and shut the door. "What in the hell are you doing? Open my door, Rene. You and I don't need to be behind nobody's closed doors." The way she tapped her pen on her desk and bit the corner of her lip, he knew he made her feel uneasy, but he didn't care.

He walked over to her desk, determined to get her back. Palms flat on her desk, he leaned in to speak to her. "Listen, I know I fucked up, and I know you hate me, and I know what I did to you and Laurie was low, but I miss you, Mia. Baby, please, I want to be with you. I can't sleep and when I'm with her, I wish I was with you. It's like you have me under some kinda fucking spell and no matter how many hours, days or weeks go by, I can't get over you, Mia," he spoke genuinely. He stood there looking into her eyes, waiting for her to tell him she needed him too and missed him just as much and wanted him back, but she just stared at him. "Mia, baby, please say something. Tell me I'm not the only one feeling this way. You said you loved me too. Baby, please," he begged.

She sighed and then removed her glasses. "I don't know what to tell you or what you want to hear me say, but this is over, we are over. After you and your little Mrs. came at me in Vegas like Will and Jada, I knew you were there to stay. I can't deal with you or Laurie, and please tell her she can stop showing up at this office to spy on me. I'm not interested in your two-timing ass. I have a man who is single, committed, romantic as fuck and breaks my fucking back on a daily basis, so please save your words because they mean absolutely nothing to me, Rene.

"You will never touch me—," she tried to say, but he covered her lips with his. It was a risky move, but he couldn't control himself. She jerked away and then slapped the shit out of him. He was shocked, and he knew then that he had really hurt her. She pushed back from her desk and stood. "You chose your *wife*, now go to her and enjoy your motherfucking choice! Stay the fuck away from me!" she spat and wiped her mouth as if his kiss was one of the nastiest kisses she'd ever tasted. She stormed out of her office with no more words.

Rene stood there for a few moments feeling defeated. His eyes burned, and his heart ached because he had it bad for Mia. He was truly in his feelings and didn't know how he could just let her go. Before he could exit her office, his cell rang. He pulled it from his pocket and cringed when he saw *Wifey* on the screen. He wasn't in the mood to talk to her at that moment, but he answered the ball and chain.

"Hey, baby, what's going on?" he asked as headed to the door. He wanted to vacate Mia's office as quickly as possible.

"Is this a bad time, baby?"

"No, not at all, Laurie, what's up?"

"Well, I have news," she announced with excitement in her voice.

"You have news? I hope it's good," Rene said, trying his best not to sound dry.

"I think it is," she said. He could hear the smile in her voice.

Not particularly interested, he appeased her. "Well, are you going to share it? I mean, you're not calling in the middle of the afternoon to talk recipes," he joked. If she could see his face, she'd see that he couldn't care less what her news was.

"Baby, we are pregnant!" she squealed.

Rene stopped in his tracks. "What?" he blurted, hoping she heard excitement and not *what the fuck?* like he meant.

"Yes, baby, you heard me right. We are pregnant!"

"Oh my God, Laurie. Are you serious? How do you know? Fill me in," he said. He rushed into his office and fell back onto the sofa. He had no strength to make it to his desk. The news was too much, and he began to perspire.

"Well, I had been feeling a little nauseous, but that wasn't the red flag. I noticed I hadn't had my cycle in seven weeks, so I grabbed a test, and it's positive."

"Oh, wow, baby. I am speechless!"

"I know, and I know this news is out of left field, but this is just what we need. God is for this marriage, baby, and this is a good thing, right?"

He paused, but unwillingly agreed. He felt that this was a horrible thing. Punishment from God. "It is, baby, and I'm just blown away," he said truthfully because this was the last thing he wanted to hear. Laurie had been on birth control since their last kid because post-partum had whipped her ass, and they both had agreed on no more kids.

"I made an appointment to see the doctor. After we get the confirmation from him, we'll tell the kids."

"That sounds like a plan," he recited like a robot. The fake excitement voice was now programmed into his body. Now everything was usually fake around Laurie, not genuine at all.

"Okay, baby. I love you," she sang.

"I love you too," he said and ended the call. He put the phone down by his side and tried to gather his thoughts. How in the fuck could he leave now? His wife was pregnant with their third kid, leaving would be a horrible decision. "Fuck, fuck, fuck!" he spat. His jaws tightened, and his temples flared. He wanted Mia. Mia was the one he wanted to father another child with. He was all in his feelings over Mia, not Laurie, so why did she have to be pregnant? "Lord, God, we ain't tight, I know, but for real…this of all things, Lord? Where is the mercy for a brother?" he said, and there was a tap on his door.

He snapped out of his zone and straightened his face. Whoever it was on the other side of the door had no concerns with his personal business, so he put his home issues on mute. "Come in," he called out. When the doors opened, he was shocked to see Mia. "Mia, what, what—," he stuttered. He was astounded to see her.

She walked in and shut the door behind her. She took a stand right in front of him, inches away, and the scent of her perfume drove him insane.

"I don't want shit from you, Rene. You need to stay with Laurie because I could never marry a man like you. All I want from you is your dick. No strings, no dates, no romance, just your dick. Head of course, but this is purely physical," she established. She stood there waiting on him to speak, but he didn't want to agree to those terms. He loved Mia and wanted more, but to have her back, he reluctantly accepted.

"If that's how you want it," his baritone voice confirmed.

"Yes, that is how I want it. I am involved, and I like what I have with my man. You have Laurie, and I'm not sure what the fuck goes on in Winters-land, but I don't give a flying fuck. All I know is my body misses you, Rene, and I can't sleep. When I'm making love to him flashes of you invade my brain, so I only want your dick, you got it? Don't send me no fucking flowers, don't ask me out for a meal and don't buy me one damn gift. All I want from you is some good dick! I want to cum like I used to cum. I want you to fuck me in my ass and make me shake all over," she purred.

His dick swelled, and he knew she could see it. He wanted to grab her, throw her onto the sofa and fuck her right then and there, but since she was the one spewing out orders, she'd be the one to make the first move. "I will give you what you want, Mia. I want more than that and you know it, but given the circumstances, neither of us can so I'll be happy to fuck you when and wherever you want to be fucked. You have no idea how bad I want to take you right now, but if sex is all you want, I'm good with that."

"Good," she said and then leaned in and gave him a wet and sexy kiss. "I'd liked to have you right now too, but I have work to do. We will only communicate by email. No text, no calls."

"I'm fine with that," Rene said and stood. He stood close enough for their lips to touch again. "You know I want more, but for now I'll take whatever I can get to feel you again."

"And no more talk about what you want. It's fucking annoying."

"Understood," he said and kissed her softly. She let his tongue enter her mouth, and the moans during their kiss let him know she had missed him too. He wanted to hike up her skirt and shove his dick inside of her so bad, but he pulled back. "So that there are no secrets between us, Laurie just told me she's pregnant," he confessed.

Mia laughed. "I don't give a fuck. I don't want you, nor do I want to walk in her shoes. All I want is for you to fuck me over and over again. All I want is to feel your dick inside of my pussy and deep inside of my ass. I want to ride your face until I cream. All I want to do is share sexual escapades with you. I want you to pull my hair, slap my ass and make me call out your name, that's it, Rene Winters. Are we clear?"

"As a bell," he replied.

"I'll make reservations for tonight. Find a way to get the fuck out of the house. I know you just got word she's knocked up, so you may want to leave early to celebrate with her if you want this pussy. If you don't show, you won't get another opportunity to fuck me. I'll email you the details," she said over her shoulders as she went for the door. She paused when she grabbed the knob and turned to him.

"What?" he asked, but she said nothing, just gave him a smile and then vacated his office.

Excited and ready, he took her advice and left work early. He headed over to Laurie's office with flowers and took her to dinner. He took her home, they spent a little time with the kids before putting them down and he gave her a story about having to go back to the office. He swore he wouldn't be long and told her that because he dipped out of work early to celebrate the pregnancy, he had to go back. He checked his email and went straight to the location that Mia sent to him. He got the key from the front desk and when he opened the door, Mia was ass naked and ready.

They started with small talk and drinks, and Mia reminded him that they weren't friends, only fuck buddies. After she shut him up, she undressed him and straddled his face first. He had missed her scent and her essence, and she rode his mouth with ease. Before she released, she flipped over and took him inside of her mouth while he continued to devour her pussy. Mia's head game was wicked, so he had to focus on pleasing her and not erupting in her face. It was something about Mia that made him weak. Laurie wasn't ugly and was still so beautiful to him, but Mia had elegance about herself, and her bedroom game was genuine and natural.

Most times Rene felt that Laurie was putting on a show, like a circus animal doing tricks for applause, but with Mia it was different. She made him feel like he was a king, like he was the master of love making, and that he missed.

"I'm going to fucking cum, baby, aaahhh, aaahhh, ooohhh," Mia moaned and rolled her hips in a circular motion as he held on to her tightly. He welcomed her juices and licked and lapped up every drop. He slid his tongue inside of her opening looking for more because he wanted this woman and hated she was no longer his.

She repositioned her body to the side of him and continued to suck his dick. It felt good as fuck, but he wanted to fuck her. He wanted to feel her walls and penetrate her insides so he could feel like she was his. "Baby, un-uh, I wanna fuck you. Come on and ride this dick, baby," he demanded, and she got into position. She came down on him slowly, but he raised his hips because he was so anxious to feel her tight walls. Mia hadn't had kids yet, so he figured that's why she felt more snug than Laurie, and the snugger the fucking better. When she worked her hips on him, he went numb like a bitch. His toes curled and within minutes, he nutted all up in her. Never had he nutted so quickly with her. He just missed her, and he missed her pussy.

"Baby, I'm so sorry. It's just been a while and your pussy—,"

"Don't, Rene, don't explain. I already know," she said, placing two fingers over his lips. "I shouldn't be here. I shouldn't be fucking with you, Rene, but the truth is, I love fucking you. My man is everything. We had a hiccup but now we are good, and I don't want to mess that up. He just doesn't fuck me like you do. Don't get me wrong, I love making love to my man, and it's good, but with you it's great. I tried to stay away. I tried to let it go. I tried to get over you, and I have let you go from my heart, but I'm still caught up on your sex. I'm in my feelings over dick, not over you, so don't get this shit twisted. You are not a good person. Hell, neither am I, but for this reason only, we are good. I have forgiven you for what you did to me, but I don't want you. As long as I'm fucking you, my world is complete because I'll have all that I need."

Rene said nothing. He had to admit that his fucking feelings were hurt. He fucking loved this woman, and all she wanted was VIP access to his dick. He started to say no, fuck this, he didn't want to be her boy toy, but his dick was rising again, so he put his feelings to the fucking side and wore her pussy out.

By the time they left the hotel, neither of them was walking straight. He drove home with a big smile plastered on his cheating face. "You think this is over, Mia? Not by a long shot. I'm going to make you mine, baby, and that motherfucker, Morris, don't stand a damn chance," Rene declared as he turned onto his block.

Getting pregnant was a nice try, he thought when he thought about Laurie, but he knew he could be a good father married or divorced. Rene loved and wanted Mia Collins, and his plan was to have her by any means.

Chapter Nineteen

Omari

He sat in his truck staring at her door. He didn't want to see Victoria, but he had to talk to her because he could be her child's father. "Fuck, man, just get out of the truck," he told himself, but didn't open the door. He didn't know what was holding him back, but he did not want to deal with the situation. *It's never a good time to deal with it*, he thought and then opened the door. He had no clue what he would say to her or how she would even react, but Morris was right. It was time to stop ignoring her.

She hadn't acted alone, and he was just as much to blame for how things went down. If he hadn't betrayed Morris and kept his dick in his pants, they would all still be good. Their growing business would still be thriving, and he'd have his friend back. He shut the car door and headed up to her front door. When he rang the bell, he wished he hadn't, but it was too late to turn back. Omari was well over six feet and a manly man, but he felt like a little boy awaiting an ass whippin' by his father for doing something he had no business. "I can't do this," he said and was about to head for his truck, but the door opened to a short and very pregnant Victoria. He looked at her for a moment and noticed that her cute nose had spread, and the area of her neck and upper chest were darker than what he'd remembered, but she still looked beautiful. "Hey," he said, breaking the silence.

"Hey is all you got?" she snapped

"Listen, Vicki, it was hard enough for me to show up here. Please don't make it harder for me."

She sighed and held her swollen belly with one hand. She bit down on her bottom lip and then shook her head. "Listen, I don't care to hear shit about how hard it was for you to come here, Omari. We fucked! *We* … Not just myself, but we, and in the process, *we!*" she yelled, "made a baby. And as sad as all this is for you, it's worse for me because I'm the one with the evidence of shame everywhere I fucking go. So don't you show up to my muthafuckin' doe' talkin' bout how hard shit is. I lost everything, Omari, everything! I'm living with my eighty-four-year-old grandmother, when I used to live in a mini-fucking-mansion.

"You lost a friend, that's it, Omari. You lost Morris and still walked away with half of your business, so please spare me. I am seven and a half months pregnant with your baby, not Morris' baby, and I know you know this, you muthafuckin' coward. When I conceived this baby, Morris was in Cali surveying land, so please spare me!" she spat. The tears were now rolling down her cheeks, and he felt bad because no matter how he tried to deny it, she was right.

He cleared his throat. "Vicki, are you certain? Are you one-hundred percent sure?"

"If I'm eight and a half months, no. If I am six and a half months, no, but I know seven and a half months ago that Morris was on a trip," she said.

"Then why did you lie to Morris?" he asked.

"What? Are you fucking serious?" she said and stepped out onto the porch. "I lied because I was too busy trying to save my marriage. I lied because I wanted my husband to forgive me and stay with me and father this child. I lied because you jumped fucking ship when the shit hit the fan, Omari. You were man enough to fuck me up against the wall, in my hot tub and all over my husband's got'damn house, but as soon as shit got real, you acted as if you didn't know me. Who fucking does that?

"You want to know why I lied? I lied for me because you didn't have my back, you bastard!" she belted. Her words cut like a knife. She was more than right. She was spot on, and he felt like a low-down bastard. He never loved Victoria, but he carried a flame for her. It started out as sex, and that was it. Yes, he was attracted to her in every way, and she was a plus-sized goddess, but he never wanted to be her husband, her man and damn sure not her child's father. Now, he was staring the truth in the face, and he had to do something good about it.

"Listen, Vicki. I'm sorry," he said.

She clicked her tongue and folded her arms. "I don't believe that shit, Omari. Why now? Why are you showing up now?"

"Because it's the right thing to do."

"Says fucking who? I know damn well your simple ass didn't come up with that on your own. I called and texted and even came by yo' place a million times, so why fucking now?" she demanded.

"A friend of mine told me I was being an asshole," he admitted, omitting Legacy's name.

"Your friend was right," Victoria agreed.

"Listen, it's a bit cool out here. Can we go inside?" he asked.

"No, because my grandma might shoot you," she said.

"Damn, it's that serious?"

"Yes muthafucka, it's that serious, but the baby is hungry though," she said.

"Whatever the baby wants, we'll get."

"So, you're agreeing to take me to get a bite to eat?" she asked suspiciously.

"Yes, go grab a jacket and we can go talk about our kid, and you can fill me in on what I missed."

"Oh, Lord, that will take longer than dinner."

"That's fine, Vicki, and after we talk, we can make arrangements for you to be in your own place. I have a few vacant units, so you don't have to worry. I will right my wrong."

She smiled. "Omari, don't say shit you don't mean. You've made tons of promises in the past and when shit hit the fan, you got ghost. I can't take that shit anymore. Not now while I'm carrying this little boy."

He grabbed his chest. "It's a boy?"

"Yes, it's a boy," she confirmed with an easy smile.

"Oh shit, I'm going to have a son?"

"Looks like it," she confirmed.

"Go grab yo' jacket. We got a lot of catching up to do," he said, and she went inside. As soon as she was on the other side of the door, he texted Legacy.

Thanks u were right

I'm always right, but about what?

Going to see Victoria

Really, did she cuss u the fuck out and send u away cryin like a bish

Hahaha, u funny, no we bout 2 go eat

Good Omari I wish u the best

Thanks

Anytime my friend

Victoria came back to the porch with a designer jacket and handbag. After she locked the door, Omari wanted to comment, but he didn't. "So, you can still rock Gucci, even though yo' man left you penniless?" he said after they both climbed into his truck.

"For yo' info, Omari, Morris didn't take my clothes, shoes, handbags or etc. He allowed me to keep all of my personals, but there is no alimony, promise of child support or anything of that nature. I don't want your fucking money,

Omari. I just want you to take care of your child and be a got'damn father," she spat.

"Listen, I'm sorry, okay? I didn't mean shit by it. I just had to ask. I mean, you keep stressing me about not having money and shit, so I just asked."

"I don't have money, and I can't work because I'm too far along. I get some assistance now, but very damn little in case you're wondering. My gran is on a fixed fucking income, so although I crave graham crackers and chocolate, I can't afford them. I can't make midnight snack trips when I crave, so there. I just need you to fucking be here. Not so I can ball out or have shopping sprees at the fucking mall, but for once when I want some ice cream, I don't have to ask my neighbor's kids if they momma got some in their fucking freezer!" she cried.

Omari looked at her tears and felt like shit. He had lost a friend, but financially he was doing damn well, and that Victoria was going through this because of their affair made him feel like shit. "Look, I'm sorry, and I can't say that shit enough. From this day forward, I got you. After I feed you and the baby, I will take you to my building near Lake Shore and show you the two units I have with two bedrooms. You pick the unit you want and then tomorrow we go shopping for furniture. When you get home tonight, I want you to sleep easy, okay?

"I'll have a few guys come through tomorrow to pack up all your shit, and then I will take you to your new place. It's been over five months since I've done the right thing, Vicki. I want my kid to have a nice home. If you crave ice-cream, graham crackers or whatever, you call me or text me. Until our baby is born and you are good to go back to work, I'll take care of you," he said sincerely. She didn't get pregnant alone, and he didn't blame Morris for leaving her anymore because had it been his wife, he'd have done the same thing.

"What about us, Omari?" she sighed with her head hung low.

He paused. "Right now, I honestly don't know. I enjoyed fucking around with you and at the time I was very attracted to you, but now I don't know."

She looked out the window. "It is what it is, right?"

"For now," he replied.

"Okay, and thank you for everything. I am tired of living here, and I need my own place. If you can hold us down until I can get back to work, I'd appreciate it. That's way more than I expected."

"I'm just trying to make up. I was wrong for leaving you out in the cold."

"Yes, the fuck you were," she laughed. "Now, let's go. I'm so hungry right now, and the baby is doing somersaults."

"He's moving?" he asked.

"Yes, and he won't stop."

"Can I?" he asked, reaching for her belly.

She paused and then smiled. "Sure, go ahead." Omari placed a hand on her tummy, but she guided his hand to the right spot, and he pulled back when he felt the baby kick hard. "What's wrong?" she asked.

"Nothing, nothing at all. It just felt funny."

"Imagine how I feel. Sometimes he kicks so hard that it hurts."

"He's already my little athlete," Omari smiled.

"I guess," she answered. Omari pulled out of her grandmother's driveway, and they chatted and debated on what to eat. Since Victoria was the one with child, she won him over and they hit up a pizza joint. They talked, laughed and Victoria showed him a video on her phone of the baby's ultrasound. Omari was blown away, and he felt obligated to make better decisions for his unborn child. All the drama and avoiding Victoria was wrong on so many levels and just sitting and talking to her, he owned up to his foolish decisions. He promised that he would help her in any way he could, but he could not promise her a relationship, something he knew she wanted him to commit to. He was still feeling Legacy and still hoping that he and Legacy got together. Yes, he was in his feelings over Legacy, but what could he do, feelings were not a light switch.

After they ate and sat in the restaurant and talked forever, Victoria decided she was too tired to look at the apartments that night and they agreed to go the next day. When he took Victoria back to her place, he gave her a tight squeeze and thanked her for not kicking him off her porch. As promised, he picked her up the next day and took her to one of his buildings, and she chose the apartment she wanted to call home. They did some furniture shopping, and he took her to a few different stores for cookware, dishes, towels, curtains and other household essentials.

He took her to the grocery store and didn't say a word about all the fatty items he thought were unhealthy for her and the baby that she added to the cart. They unloaded, and he took her back to her grandmother's since the furniture was scheduled to be delivered in a couple of days. He built up the courage to go inside to meet her grandmother. He was grateful he made it out alive because for a woman that old, she had fire in her belly and as fit as Omari was, he was sure her grandmother could take him.

"So, you'll pick me up on Thursday bright and early, right? You know the furniture delivery is between nine and twelve," she said.

"How about you go to my place and stay, and then I don't have to get up as early?"

"Omari, that's sweet and thanks, but no. I don't want any mixed signals, and I don't want things to get complicated. I let go, and I can't subject my heart to any more pain. I'm over that."

"I'm not asking you to sleep with me, Vicki. All I'm saying is it would be better if you were at my place. It's closer to your new pad, less traffic, and you know how I feel about mornings."

She was quiet. He gave her a few moments to process the idea. "Okay, fine, Omari. Can you allow me to pack a bag and tell my grand where I'll be?"

"Of course," he replied with a smile. After Victoria packed a bag and said goodnight to her grandmother, she and Omari headed to his place. They made a quick stop because the baby had to have a Pizza Puff and then they went to his place. Omari had a one-bedroom bachelor pad, so that meant one bed, and he could tell Victoria was uneasy.

"It's a Cal King," he said. "There's plenty of room."

"I know, but…" she sighed.

"But what, Vic? Come on."

"It's been a long time since I slept next to a man. I know I'm almost eight months, but my pussy still works, and it still gets hot, so maybe I should sleep on the sofa."

"Nonsense. I can't have my baby on an uncomfortable couch, so you take the bed," he said.

"Are you sure?"

"No, but you can't sleep on the couch. What kinda man would I be if I let you do that?"

"A horrible one," she joked. He snatched a pillow from the bed, and she climbed in. He grabbed the throw from his chair that sat it the corner of his room, and she stopped him. "Omari," she said. He paused in his tracks. "I'd rather you stay here and sleep with me."

He turned to her. "But I thought you said..."

"I know what I said, but this bed is enormous. We can share it."

"Are you sure, because a second ago you were saying the exact opposite?"

"Yes, I am sure," she said and patted the bed. He walked back and climbed in, making sure he got comfortable on one side.

"You can come closer," she encouraged.

He hesitated, but moved closer. He spooned her and then rubbed her swollen belly. "I guess he's asleep?" he said because he didn't feel any kicks or movement.

"Yes, he's settled in." They lay quiet for a while and then she took his hand and moved it up to her breasts. Instinctively, he massaged them, and her moans brought back memories. Although he thought it would be best if they didn't have sex, his dick told him to smash. Within moments, he was deep inside of her, and it was even better than he remembered. It was tighter and wetter, and he couldn't get enough. She begged him for rest and reminded him that the load in front of her was heavy.

He finally released the nut he tried desperately to hold on to and allowed her to get some rest. The next morning, he hit it again before he left for work. He wasn't sure what they were getting themselves into, but he promised himself that he would never abandon her again.

Chapter Twenty

Reynard

Rey was sitting in his office looking over the delinquent accounts, and there was a knock on the door. "Come in." His eyes bulged when she walked into his office because she was the last person he expected to see walking through the door. "Joss, what are you doing here? Is Lisa okay?"

"Relax, Rey. Lisa is fine. She told me you worked here, so I put it in my GPS and stopped by."

"For what?" he asked. He barely said two words to her at the house, so why would she want to stop by his job?

"Just to chat, say hello. You act like you're afraid to say two words to me at the house, so I figured if we were alone, maybe you'd at least try to get to know me. I'm sure you're interested in getting to know me better."

"Why would I want to get to know you better, Joss? You will only be in town for a short while. The less we speak the better because I know how y'all chicks are, and I don't need no drama with Lisa. We are good, so sorry, *cuz*, we don't need to get to know each other," he said bluntly. Joss looked like trouble, smelled like trouble and the sway in her hips when she walked was double trouble, and Rey wanted to make sure she didn't get any ideas.

"Wow, okay. So, you are gay?"

"Excuse me!" he shot her.

"Am I wrong? When Lisa said you weren't gay, I was like, bitch please! If that nigga fucks wit' yo' ass, dat nigga gay," she laughed out loud.

"Joss, you don't know shit about me, and nobody asked yo' ass to come up in my office with this noise, so see yo' way the fuck out," Rey growled. That bitch didn't know a motherfucking thing about him, and he was not gay.

"Hold on, hold on, dude," she said and took a seat. "I'm not here to throw no shade. I love my cuzzo like a sister and shit, but we both know Lisa was born with a dick, so please explain to me why you don't consider yourself to be a homosexual? Dude, I live in Atlanta, so you can be honest with me, unless you're bi?" she quizzed.

"What does it matter, Joss? Why are you so concerned about my sexual preferences?"

She paused and then her lips curled into a smile. "You have to ask, Rey?" He just looked at her awaiting her answer. "Well, if you want me to just spit it out, I'll spit it out. You my type. I'm not trying to take you from my cousin, I just would like to share you while I'm in town. You know, get some of yo' sexy ass dick." He burst into laughter. "What the fuck is so funny, Rey? You think I'm some silly ass bitch who likes to tell jokes or some shit?"

"Nope, I just think it's funny how you'd think I'd be like, that's cool, that sounds like a plan. Sure, we can fuck!"

"Boy, please. Don't sit here like you are some fucking saint. I know you was living with a chick when you hooked up with my cousin, so cut the shit because I know you ain't the faithful type," she said using air quotes. "Now, whether you know it or not, I've seen you looking at me, and I know you want to sample some of this. I won't tell if you won't. We both know you can't sample Lisa's new man-made pussy for what, another two, maybe three weeks? I just opened the door for you to get some good pussy, and if you with it, I'm with it is all I'm saying," she said, rubbing her manicured finger down the center of her breasts.

Rey stayed seated because his dick was rock hard. He wasn't gay, he loved women and could never touch a burly ass man and hated that people assumed he was gay if they knew that Lisa was transgender. "Well, thanks for the invitation, but I'll pass. You can see yourself out," he said and turned back to his computer. He clicked his mouse, but she didn't budge. "Is there something else you need?" he asked.

She stood. "For now no, but trust, this won't be the last time you see my face."

"Duhhh, you will be at the house when I get off, right?" he joked.

"Ha, ha, ha, Rey. You know what the fuck I mean. I'll be sure to wear something that I know you might like, so you can keep staring at my ass when I walk by. Ain't nobody stupid, Rey. I know you wanna fuck. You can play hard to get all you want, but I know I'll be riding that dick soon enough," she said before leaving.

As soon as she shut the door, Rey let out a deep breath. He knew he was dead fucking wrong because he could wear her pussy out. He grabbed his dick because it ached so damn bad. He needed some pussy. He was horny as fuck, and he knew if Joss continued to temp him, it could be a bad situation because he'd show her ass that he was all man. He wasn't gay. Lisa was a woman, and that was the end of the fucking story he declared and then stood. He readjusted his rod in his pants because it was throbbing. He wanted to release, he needed to bust one, but he didn't want to jack off in his office. "Fuck, Lisa, fuck!" he grunted in frustration.

He decided he'd take a break, run home and shove his dick down Lisa's throat because that was all Lisa could give him right now. His area down below was always in discomfort, so he didn't want to try anal at all, and Rey tried to be understanding but he was losing patience. Well, his dick was. He grabbed his phone.

Hey babe, he texted Lisa.

What's up babe

Not too much, jus feeling some type of way…need some head

Really Rey???

Yes really, if I swing by the house can you handle this for me. I'm on 10

Fuck no! I just got done with my stupid ass painful dilation and dick is the last thing on my fuckin mind

Rey paused and just looked at his phone. He knew Lisa's dilations were painful and the worst for him, but he was pissed that it would cause him not to bust one off.

R u serious bae. u no I need it in the worst way .

What the fuck eva Rey

Baby don't be like dat

Boy bye!!!

Rey didn't text back. He was pissed, and he knew he'd say some shit to get his ass kicked out. What he did do was get back on his computer. He loved and cared for Lisa and all that jazz, but he decided he needed some space. It was time to look for his own place. Lisa had her ho ass cousin from Atlanta now, so he needed his own spot because moving out of NeNe's right into Lisa's was never the plan. He grabbed his phone before doing a search and hoped she answered.

"What!" she answered.

"Hey," he said.

"What in the fuck do you want?"

"I need your help," he said.

"My help? Are you fucking serious?"

"Dead serious. This call ain't about us. I know and understand that there is no more us."

"So what do you want, Rey?"

"I need to find a place."

She laughed. "And you're calling me to help you as if I'd say yes?"

"Well, I was hoping you could at least recommend someone."

"I'll text you Camille's number, she does rentals as well. Now don't ever call me again!" NeNe said and ended the call.

Disappointed that she wouldn't help him personally, he was relieved she at least referred someone. He knew Lisa would be angry, but it was all moving so fast. The sex change, the cheating and the drama, Rey was overwhelmed, and it hadn't hit him until that very moment. "What in the fuck did I do?" he asked himself. "I'm not gay. I love Lisa, and I don't want to be with men. Why is this happening to me?" he questioned out loud.

Happy that his dick had gone down, he tried to get back to work. He got an alert from NeNe with Camille's info, and he said he'd get with her after he finished his work on the overdue accounts. Before the end of the day, he called Camille. They spoke briefly about budget and wish list, and she emailed him a credit application. He took his time and filled it out and then faxed it back to her. She promised she'd get back to him the next day after she got his results back to see what he qualified for. With that, Rey called it a day and headed home. When he got there, Joss was in the kitchen doing what she did best, which was cooking.

She looked and behaved like a ho, but her cooking skills were off the charts. "Evening, Rey," she spoke. He gave her a nod and continued towards the bedroom since he didn't find Lisa on the sofa. He walked in to find Lisa standing in the mirror in his underwear.

"Hey," Rey spoke.

"Hey, baby," Lisa purred. "Please tell me the truth. Do I look fat to you?"

"Lisa, baby, please don't even start that. You have two eyes, and you can see that you're not fat."

"I feel fat. Since the surgery and not being able to work out and with Joss cooking two or three times a day, I know I'm going to be a big girl in five fucking minutes," Lisa cried.

Rey walked over to him. "Listen, stop okay? You weigh a hundred pounds wet, so stop. You are not fat, and you look perfect."

Lisa smiled. "Baby, you are always so sweet. I am tired of this, Rey. This surgery was too much and at times I regret it. The dilation is too much, and the bleeding and the constant discomfort, I just want to get past all of this pain," Lisa cried. "And not being able to please you, and I know you've been patient with me," he continued. Rey felt horrible for wanting to move and knew Lisa would not take the news well. He constantly told Rey how happy he was to have him there, so telling him he was getting his own spot would upset him even more. He was already going through enough, so Rey decided to wait for another time to tell him.

"I know it's overwhelming, and I know it's not a walk in the park, but you are a strong woman, and you will get through this. When your body heals, and you are done with the medications, dilations and doctor visits, you will be happy you did it. I am happy you did it and when all of this is healed up and ready, I am going to wear it out," he said, pulling Lisa into his arms. "I know it's hard, bae, but you are going to be amazing."

"Well, I don't feel amazing, and I think Joss is trying to fatten me up on purpose. She has always been jealous of my flat stomach, now she's plotting on my waistline," Lisa joked.

"Baby, you are not fat, so stop it. In a few weeks, you'll be able to go to the gym, but in the meantime, don't be eating up everything. Have one biscuit instead of two."

"Have you tasted that bitch's biscuits, Rey? You can't just eat one. That bitch can burn in that kitchen," Lisa said, moving over to the bed. He put on a pair of loose yoga pants and a tank.

"Yes, she can cook. You need to get a couple of lessons before she goes back to Georgia."

"Oh, I forgot to tell you," Lisa said.

"Forgot to tell me what?"

"Joss is thinking about staying."

"What? When did this happen?"

"Rey, ssshhh, lower your voice," Lisa said.

"When did she say she was thinking about staying?"

"Well, it doesn't look like it's going to work out with her and Dre, so I told her she could stay as long as she needed to."

"You said that without discussing that with me?"

"Come again?" Lisa said, putting his hands on his narrow hips.

"You know what I mean, Lisa. I live here too now."

"I know that, Rey, but at the end of the day, this is my place, and that's my family."

Family that wanna fuck yo' man, Rey started to say, but instead he said, "Okay, fine. I'm going to shower," and walked away.

"Reynard," Lisa called out, but he shut the bathroom door. Reynard knew for sure he had to get his own place because Joss was the type of chick that would get him shot, and he definitely did not want to hear Lisa reminding him that this was his house. That's something NeNe never did until the breakup and things got bad, but they made household decisions together. If it had been NeNe and one of her relatives, she would have discussed with him first instead of throwing her hands on her hips telling him whose house it was.

"Yes, this is for the motherfucking birds. I got to get my own spot," he said and then stepped into the shower.

Chapter Twenty-One

Anika

After hours of begging, NeNe decided she'd go to the funeral with Jaxson. She felt he should go alone, but he insisted that she be with him. Since the day of Michelle's mother death, she was calling Jaxson every other hour, and he had spent a lot of time with her and her family. NeNe tried not to trip because legally they were still married, and she was sure if her momma died and she wasn't involved with Jaxson she'd probably lean on Reynard for support too. She couldn't wait for the funeral to be over and for Jaxson's divorce to be final so they could rid themselves of Michelle because Michelle was on NeNe's last nerve.

"Baby, are you hungry?" Jaxson asked NeNe, bringing her back to the room. Her mind was on a million and one things, and that included Michelle.

"A little, but not much. I had a late lunch after I showed my last house."

"Well, I'm going to run out for some wings, do you want some?"

"From where, babe?"

"Hooters."

"Yes, I could go for some wings from Hooters. Get me an eight-piece Chipotle Garlic," NeNe said.

"That's it? Do you want fries or a drink?"

"You know what, get me some onion rings."

"Okay," he said and went over and gave her a quick kiss. "I'll be back soon."

"Okay," she said. He left, and she grabbed the remote. A few moments later, she noticed his phone on the coffee table, so she grabbed it and ran to the door but he was already gone. "Shit," she said and went back inside. She put it back the coffee table and then a few minutes later, it rang. The screen said *Micky*, and she wondered what she needed that time. "Stop calling my man, you trick," NeNe said to the phone, and then it finally stopped ringing. A second later, she called again, and NeNe wanted so badly to answer but she was just a girlfriend, not a wife. After it finally stopped, a text message alert came through. NeNe tried to resist and respect Jaxson's privacy, but she grabbed his phone and to her surprise, there was no lock code on the phone. She clicked a few icons and went to his messages. She went to Michelle's message and her hand shook, but she clicked to see what was there.

She knew it was bad to be in his phone, but fuck it, she was already too far gone to not read. She scrolled back a few days and was happy to find that the messages weren't bad, but she wasn't happy with Michelle mentioning her name. She had messages that read, ***Please come and do this, if your new chick will let you out*** or ***If NeNe loosens her riggings on you.*** NeNe had never stopped Jaxson from going where he wanted to go. NeNe kept scrolling and paused when she read, ***I miss u so much JT & I'm so sorry. I wish we could start over again.***

I miss u 2 Micky, but I've moved on

She will never love u like I love u

Maybe so, but I still love and want to be with her

NeNe smiled. At least Jaxson wasn't low-down like Rey and doing foul shit behind her back. She read a few more messages and continued snooping in his phone. She went through his pictures and even though there were still pictures of Michelle in his album, she didn't get mad. After peeping in his emails and going to his Facebook messages, she put his phone down. Jaxson was one of the good ones, so she exhaled. There were no traces of other women in his phone other than Michelle, and she was grateful.

When Jaxson walked in the door, she raced to greet him with a hug. "Baby, can I at least put the food down," he kidded.

"My bad, let me help you," she said, taking one of the packages.

"Did I leave my phone here?" he asked, looking around.

"Yes, it's over on the coffee table."

"Good. I was hoping it was here."

They put the bags on the peninsula. "Yes, you did, and I have a confession."

"You went through my phone, didn't you?"

"I did, and I'm sorry. I know that was wrong, but Michelle called, and then she texted. I'm sorry," NeNe said. After hearing what she had done out loud, she felt ashamed.

"Come here," he said and pulled her close. "That was a bad thing to do because that's an invasion of privacy and shows me that you don't trust me, but I'm glad you did."

"Come again?"

"I'm glad because hopefully now you can trust me. Now that you see I have nothing to hide from you, maybe you'll relax and just let me love you," he said and kissed her.

"I trust you, JT, but I don't trust Michelle. I know her momma died, but I'm not comfortable with you just running to be by her side. I'm sorry she lost her mom, but you two are no longer together, so she has to deal with some things on her own, baby. And with her putting 'I miss you's' out there, it makes me feel some kinda way."

"I hear you, NeNe, and I promise you that I'm only there helping with comforting her. Yes, I have held her, yes I've been her shoulder to cry on, but I'm doing those things because I am a good person, and I loved her mother too. I don't flirt, I don't kiss, I don't engage in anything with Micky other than just being there to support her. She knows we are over, and she knows I'm in love with you, so don't worry. The funeral is day after tomorrow and once her mother is laid to rest, our lives will go back to normal."

"Can you do me one more favor, JT?"

"Whatever you want, baby."

"Can you get her things out of the garage? Get her a storage unit, I don't care, until the divorce is final. I don't want you anywhere near her."

"Done," Jaxson said. "It's all about me and you, and I want you to always feel safe and confident that I have your best interests at heart. Micky and I had our chance, and we blew it, now I'm taking my chances with you," he smiled.

"Well, you chose wisely, and I will make you happy."

"And I will hold you to that. Now, let's eat before this food gets cold."

"Yes, let's eat." After they ate, they sat outside in the backyard and enjoyed a few glasses of wine. It was early October and a bit cool, but Jaxson had a fire pit. He got the fire going, and they reclined the lounge chairs and talked about everything and nothing. NeNe felt like she had met the man of her dreams and in a few short months, she had fallen deeper in love with Jaxson than she had ever loved Reynard. Jaxson was easy going, slow to anger and so fun to be with. They never had a dull moment, and even just exchanging childhood stories by the fire pit they were super happy together.

She was telling Jaxson about the time she waited in line for nine hours to get New Edition tickets when his phone rang. He picked it up, and she said, "Michelle?"

"Yes," he said.

"Go ahead. It might be important."

"You sure?"

"Baby, just answer," she insisted.

"Yeah," he said after he answered. "Not really, what's up?" he said. NeNe could hear a lot of noise from Michelle's end, and then Jaxson put the call on speaker.

"Uncle Jessie and Uncle Pete made it, and everybody is asking about you, JT. They want to see you," Michelle said.

"Micky, I can't. NeNe and I are pretty much in for the night," Jaxson said.

"Who gives a damn about yo' new woman, JT? The family is here, and you're still family, so you should come by to see everybody. TiTi done cooked up some fish and spaghetti, and you know not everyone knows that we are separated, so do me a favor and come by here. Just stay for an hour, that's all I'm asking. I'm sure your little girlfriend will let you out for an hour," Michelle said. The noise had disappeared, so NeNe was sure she went into another room to speak frankly with Jaxson.

NeNe looked at him and mouthed the words, "Just go, babe."

He shook his head. "Like I said, Micky, not tonight. NeNe and I are in. I'll try to swing by tomorrow."

"Are you fucking serious, JT? You know momma would be so disappointed in you. You letting some new ass keep you away from family!" Michelle barked.

"*Michelle!*" Jaxson said firmly. "You cannot call me at fucking nine o'clock at night and expect me to just hop in my car and come running to you. Those days are over, we are over, and it has absolutely nothing to do with NeNe being here. You know the reasons why we split, and all the things you've done to us, to me, in this marriage. Enough is enough, and I don't have to deal with your shit at all if I choose not to for some of the things you've done to ruin our marriage. If I have time, I will come by tomorrow to see the family. Stop fronting and tell yo' people the true reason we are getting a damn divorce, and stop trying to make me out to be the fucking bad guy. You and I know it's the other way around." The line was quiet.

"Fine, JT," she sniffled. "I just lost my mother, and you put her before me."

He rubbed his temple with his free hand. "This is not a competition, Michelle. I just can't tonight."

"Whatever, JT," she said and ended the call.

"Oh wow," NeNe said.

"Yes, that's Michelle for you. A real fucking piece of work."

"Why did you want out, other than the reasons you told me before?"

"There are things that sometimes a man just doesn't want to share. I'm not harboring any deep dark secrets. We went through some things that she and I only know of."

"Okay, baby, I understand. I'm sorry for prying, but I'm glad she left." He looked at her. "If she hadn't, I would not have had the chance to fall in love with you."

He smiled. "That's true, and I'm happy to be in love with you too."

She smiled back at him. "You know I wouldn't have minded you going."

"I know, but I didn't want to. Her family is good people, and I'm sure there are card tables, drinks, good music and her aunt TiTi can cook her ass off. Everything TiTi touches in the kitchen turns to gold," Jaxson joked.

"I don't mind if you want to go," NeNe said again.

"Naw, baby, I want to spend the rest of my evening right here with my beautiful queen. When Micky left, I said never a-fucking-gain will I ever love another woman, but you walked into the office that morning after you had cut your hair, and you had on that red skirt and that creamy colored top that had that opening up top that just stopped to make you imagine what the cleavage looked like underneath. I gotta confess, baby. My heart raced, my nerves jumped and my dick got hard. Your legs though in them heels, I was like Anika Jones is a fox and if she was my lady, I'd treat her like silk," Jaxson said. NeNe smiled so hard, she thought her face would get stuck.

"That day I was like, if it's with her, I'll risk it all. I'll welcome another heartbreak if I have one opportunity with Anika. And when you told me that things weren't right with Reynard, I thought to myself, God is handing this woman over to me, and if there is a hair of a chance, I'm going to take it."

"Jaxson, you are melting my heart, and I know for a fact that you and I are supposed to be together. Michelle and Reynard made us even better for each other, so let's toast to our exes," she said, and he picked up his glass. They clinked glasses and sipped.

"I don't have a ring, and I didn't think I'd even be asking you this right now, but will you marry me, Anika?" he asked.

She stared at him at first and just blinked. "Say it again."

He cleared his throat. "I don't ever want to start over again, and I never want to be without you. You are not just my lover, you are my closest friend, and I want to marry you. Will you marry me?"

"Hell yes!" NeNe yelled and hopped off her lawn chair. Jaxson stood, and she leaped into his arms.

"I love you, baby."

"And I love you too," she cried.

"We can go ring shopping tomorrow."

She wiped her tears and nodded her head. "Okay, that works for me," she smiled. They rested in one lawn chair together for a while and then went inside. As soon as they reached Jaxson's bedroom, they stripped naked and sucked and fucked until their bodies were so worn and sore they couldn't move. The next day, they both called in and after breakfast, they dressed and went ring shopping. Later in the evening after Michelle blew up Jaxson's phone, he agreed to come over. TiTi had made her famous lasagna, and Jaxson was game. Glad that he made it, Michelle had a huge grin on her face when she opened the door, but that smile faded when she saw NeNe on his right arm.

Chapter Twenty-Two

LaTanya

Tanya was in the dressing room trying on maternity clothes. She was wasting money, but she planned to keep the receipts. No one knew she had lost her baby, and she was sick and tired of being home, so she planned to return to work. Even her client Chantel didn't know the outcome of that night. She planned to tell Kenny that the doctor released her on light duty, and she'd buy a stool for her station so she could get back to work because after three weeks, she was over being in her house alone every day. She had caught up on all of her shows on Hulu and Netflix, and to stay home another day would send her over the edge.

She went online and ordered two fake silicone pregnant stomachs. They were one-hundred bucks a pop, but she had to do it. Tanya wanted Kenny back, and that was the only way. They were getting closer by the day, and she knew she'd get him back. Every day her mind wondered where she'd get a baby and how. She had spent hours online researching adoption and looking for surrogate mothers, and the ultimate thing to do was fake a miscarriage before her due date. By then she would have won Kenny back, and they could grieve together. Going back to work was perfect.

She made her online purchases and then drove to a few baby stores. *If Kenny sees all the cute little baby items, that will help,* she thought and purchased items for her second room. It was time to get her man back, and she was willing to risk everything to have him.

A couple of days later she was up, dressed and had her new baby bump underneath her clothes. It looked so real that she felt likeshe was still pregnant. She examined herself in the mirror several times before she returned to her salon.

"Oh my God, look at you momma!" one of her stylists said, greeting her with a hug. The silicone felt real, so she wasn't afraid for anyone to touch her belly by accident, but she wouldn't give anyone a session of feeling her baby move, that was out of the question. "Welcome back."

"Thank you. I'm so glad to be back. Being on bed rest was the pits, and I'm so glad the doctor said I could come back to work. I still have to take it easy, no heavy lifting, but I got a stool that Kenny is bringing by later so I can sit when I need to sit and still slam some hair."

"I know that's real. Girl, we were praying for you. Chantel was in here talking about that night, and we all thought for sure the baby didn't make it."

Tanya laid a hand on her fake belly. "Well, my baby is fine, and we are good."

"I see. Now, you have a light day. I told your clients you were coming back, but today you only have six appointments."

"Six is good. I have to pace myself for my baby's sake. I'm focused on keeping it light."

"Well, whatever you need we are here," her stylist said. Within the next few minutes, more stylists filed in and greeted Tanya with hugs, kisses and welcome backs. A few touched her belly and since no one drew back quickly or detected it was fake, Tanya was confident and decided she'd let Kenny touch it. She would never lift her shirt, but she would let him touch and just say the baby must be sleep since he wouldn't feel any movements.

Kenny stopped by with the stool he assembled for her and promised he'd be by later that night to put the crib together. For the first time, she said, "Kenny, you can touch my stomach. Folks been touching it all day, so you can touch it." He placed both hands on the round surface and smiled.

"This is real."

"Of course."

He rubbed it a few times and then said, "Thank you." He leaned in and gave her fake belly a kiss and said, "Hey, it's your dad, and I can't wait to meet you."

Tanya's eyes welled, and she wondered why God took back her baby. She knew she'd break his heart, but she couldn't tell him the truth, not yet. She didn't have the strength to tell him, he would never speak to her again.

"Gon' now, Kenny. You know I'm emotional now and shit. I'm not trying to be up in here crying and shit, messing up my damn make-up," she fussed. She wanted to go to the bathroom and cry her eyes out. She wished she was still pregnant and not standing there with a silicone belly deceiving the man she loved.

"Okay, Tanya. I'm heading out. After I have dinner with the fam and get the girls down, I will come by to set up the crib."

"Don't fake me out, Kenny. Show the fuck up. The baby's room is almost done. I want to see his crib."

"His crib?" he said.

"I was going to let you know at the shower. But before my doctor gave me the okay to return to work, she did an ultrasound, something I had no idea she'd do at my appointment that day, and they confirmed it's a boy," she lied.

"It's a boy?" he said with excitement.

"Yes, Kenny. It's a boy, and keep it down, I don't want nobody else to know."

He pulled her in his arms. "Oh my God, baby, thank you. I'm so happy. I'm going to have a son," he said, holding her tight.

"That's what they said."

Kenny held her tightly, and she looked up at him. Then he did it. He kissed her. He kissed her deeply and passionately, and she welcomed it. Her center quickened, and she wanted him, but he instantly pulled back. "I'm sorry, Tanya. I'm so sorry. I got caught up. That was out of line, and I'm sorry."

"Kenny, it's okay. Relax."

"That shouldn't have happened, and I'm sorry."

"Stop, okay? We are good. No harm, no foul, and I will keep it to myself. I won't say nothing."

"Even if I make you mad, you won't say shit to Legacy?"

"I know what this is, Kenny, and if you want more, that's what I want. I know you're not leaving Legacy, and I'll deal with that."

"Look, that kiss should not have happened, and I won't do that shit to you and Legacy again. We have a child together, and that's all we'll ever have together. I won't cheat on Legacy again with you. I love her, and it wouldn't be fair to either of you," Kenny said.

Her eyes welled, but he wasn't speaking any new news, so she said, "I got to get back to work, and I'm sure you have stuff to do, so come by later and take care of the crib for me, aw'ight?"

"Okay, and Tanya, I care for you, and I love this kid. I don't want to see you hurt, and I'm sorry," he said and caressed her cheek. He touched her stomach. "Later, son," he said and then vacated her office. Tanya fell back against the wall because she had no idea what she was going to do. She loved Kenny so much and didn't want to completely lose him to Legacy, but she only had a small window of time to get him back.

"Lord, why did you take my baby?" she cried. She sat down and rubbed her fake tummy. It felt so real, and she felt like she was going insane. Never did she ever see herself in such a situation, and she just wished she had told Kenny the damn truth from jump. She sat in her office with her mind spinning, but no answers came to her. When there was a tap on her door, she knew her next client was there. She left her worries in her office and got back to work. All she could do is take it one minute, one hour and one day at a time. How she was going to get a baby boy when her term was up, and how could she fake another miscarriage were questions that had to wait until she was home, so she got to work and tried not to think about how things would eventually play out.

Chapter Twenty-Three

Legend

When he pulled into the parking space next to where his wife stood waiting for him, Legend's fist tightened. He had no plans on hitting her, but he wanted to because what she had done to him had ripped his heart out of his chest. He put the vehicle in park and hit the button to unlock her door and then grabbed his hat and placed it behind him on the seat. Normally, he would have gotten out and opened the door for her, like he does for his daughters too, but he didn't have an ounce of respect for Jackie at that moment. She stood there for a few moments before she finally reached for the handle. He figured she realized he wasn't getting out to open the door for her. She put her purse on the seat and then opened the back door and tossed her bag onto the backseat.

She climbed in and as soon as she snapped her seatbelt, she cried out, "Baby, I'm so sorry, and thank you for coming back for me."

"Don't thank me, Jackie. I didn't come for you, I came because of our children. We need to discuss a million and one things, so we are going to Lake Geneva as planned to talk about our marriage, your fucking affair and our divorce."

"Lake Geneva? Divorce? You can't mean that, Legend! That just can't be your final decision. I fucked up, yes, but please let's not think about divorce. I'm begging you," she said and reached out to grab his hand that rested on the arm rest. He snatched away.

"Don't you dare touch me, Jackie. You just had your hands all over another got'damn man, so don't touch me!" he roared. She drew back her hand and just sobbed. "I reserved a one bedroom villa for us to share our anniversary weekend in. I had planned to take you to RPM's Steak House for an early dinner and then take you away for a romantic weekend. I bought you lingerie and sexy underwear, and I wanted to pamper you this weekend, and this is what you do to me?"

"Honey, please. I know you are hurt, and I know—," she tried to say.

"No, you don't know, Jacqueline. How could you possibly know how I feel right now? Have you ever walked in on me fucking another woman? Have you ever caught me with a woman bent over my fucking desk with me ramming my dick in and out of her!" he yelled.

"No," she whimpered.

"Then you don't fucking know!" his voice blared. They were both quiet for a while, and he could see Jackie trembling like a kid on their way to get an ass whipping.

"Legend, please forgive me," she said. He said nothing. "Baby, I'm so sorry, please," she continued to plead. He wanted to say, *yes honey, I forgive you*, but his wounded heart still had a gaping hole in it, and he knew at the moment that he might never forgive her for what she had done. The tears just rolled down his face, and he couldn't hold in the hurt and anguish he felt. "We can get past this, Legend. I know we can," she sniffled. He still said nothing. He clenched the steering wheel and kept his tear-filled eyes on the road.

By the time they made it to the hotel, the sun was going down. Ordinarily, it would be a sight that they could awe about, but his heart ached so bad, he couldn't see the beauty in it. The valet opened his door, and another valet worker opened hers, and then they went for their bags.

"What's your last name, sir?" the concierge asked.

"Morgan," he replied.

"Mr. Morgan, I see you have a reservation for one of our one-bedroom villas?"

"Yes, I do."

"Okay, sir. We can get you checked in here and give you instructions on how to get to your unit. Your bags will be delivered shortly," he said. He printed out a little registration card, Legend scribbled his signature and then took the keys. The concierge gave him quick directions and a welcome package and told him there was a map of the grounds inside. With that, Legend and Jackie climbed back into his SUV and found their way to their villa.

Once inside, they saw that their bags had already been delivered. Jackie looked around and admired the space, and he walked into the living room to join her. She stood near the fire place and then moved to look out the sliding glass doors. He took a seat because he was ready to talk, but she stood gazing out at the grounds.

"This is beautiful, Legend. I can't believe you planned this for us."

"Why is that, Jackie? Every year I go out of my way to make our anniversary special, but apparently you forgot that shit when you let another man bend your ass over in your office. Today is our anniversary, Jacqueline. What the fuck were you thinking!" he yelled.

She swung around. "I wasn't fucking thinking, and today I made the worst choice of my life, and I was so wrong. You can punish me, not talk to me or whip my ass if you'd like to, but please don't leave me. Yes, I took for granted how wonderful you are and how good you are to me and our damn kids. Yes, I transformed into a heartless, evil, self-serving bitch when I let Calvin seduce me. I had a horrible moment of weakness. It was stupid, it was selfish, it was wrong and it was cruel and I'm sorry, Legend," she cried. "I'd give my life to start today over if I could," she said.

He cut her off. "No, fuck that shit, Jackie. You don't get to say I had an off fucking day! I need more than that. I need to know why. And tell me the got'damn truth. Was today the first time?" he bellowed. She blinked and more tears fell. "Was today the first time?" he asked again. She dropped her head. He stood up and moved closer to her, and he could see her trembling. "Answer me, Jacqueline."

She looked him in the eyes and said, "No, it wasn't."

"So, you lied today when you said it was only one time, right!" he yelled. "How can I even begin to forgive you if you can't tell me the truth?"

"I'll tell you the truth, baby. I will tell you everything, just please, Legend, please! I can't lose you, Legend. I love you, and I have no good reason for the affair. There are no words I can say to justify what I did. I, I, I just love you, Legend. I fucked up, baby, I did, and I am begging you to forgive me and we fix it. I'll never do it again. I swear on my life, I will never hurt you like this again. Please give me another chance, please. I will tell you everything. I will never lie to you again, please, Legend please!" she begged.

He had never seen Jacqueline cry so hard, not even when her mother died. He then began to hurt for the both of them. He was torn and didn't know what to do. He loved her beyond reason, but he had no idea how he was going to deal with her and her affair.

He grabbed her and held her, and they both cried in each other's arms. He didn't know what to do. A part of him wanted to tell her no and that all he wanted was a divorce, but that wasn't the case. He loved his wife, so he said, "Jackie, right now I don't know what I want to do. You broke my heart, and I'm not sure if I'll ever be able to trust you again. How can we have a marriage if I can't trust you?"

"Let me earn it back, please. Tonight, I want to come clean, and I'll tell you everything. Even if it hurts, I'm going to put it all out in the open. You may not believe me when I tell you, Legend, but I'm glad you caught me. I'm glad there are no more secrets, no more deceit and no more lies. I will tell you everything. After I do, it's your call. I don't want a divorce. I'll go to counseling, change my numbers, give you the passwords to my email, Facebook, Instagram, Twitter, whatever it takes. I can't live without you and my kids. You and the kids are my life, and I know I don't deserve you, just please try to forgive me," she said with desperation in her voice.

Legend wished he didn't believe her words and that he was no longer in his feelings over her cheating ass, but he was. He loved her, and he didn't want to lose her either. "If you want me to even consider staying with you, Jacqueline, you need to tell me everything. Any question I ask, I want the truth. If you lie to me about anything, I swear to you that we are done. I want to hate you, but I can't. I want to shake the shit out of you, but that won't change the fact that you cheated on me. I love you, and I know I'll never fully understand why you did it, but I need you to know that you broke something in me. I had an idea, and there were times I felt that you were untrue, but I was in denial and avoided it and hoped it wasn't true."

"Legend, I'm so sorry."

"I know." He moved over to his bag and took out a bottle of Johnny Walker Blue. It was the best, and he had to crack it open because he would need a few to handle what his wife was about to tell him. "Should I order you a bottle of wine?" he asked.

She stepped out of her shoes and walked over to the island where he stood. "No. I'll have what you're having if that's okay because I need something stronger." She went for her bag. "Do you mind if I go up and shower first?"

"No, I don't, but do me a favor."

"Anything."

"Give me your phone," he said.

She paused at first. "No problem, just brace yourself," she said and went for her purse. She took out her phone and keyed in the passcode. "If you get locked out, the password is the twins' birthday," she said before handing it over. "No more secrets and no more lies," she said and then turned to get her bag. She headed up the stairs while fixed a drink. After he filled his glass, he ran up to take his bag and then went back down. He grabbed her phone and went over to the sofa and went through her phone. He learned that Calvin was once a client she won a case for. The settlement awarded him a nice chunk of change. The messages were like any other cheater's messages. One thing Legend was relieved to know after reading over five dozen messages, Jacqueline had never once said she loved him.

By the time he sifted through her Facebook and pictures, she came back down in a long, loose fitting, spaghetti strap dress. It was one of the items he got for their trip, and she looked as beautiful as he imagined she would in it. "I looked through my bag, and thank you. Every piece you chose for me is perfect, and I love them all."

"I know your taste, Jackie."

"I know, I was just saying thank you." She made her way to the kitchen and filled the glass he left out for her with ice and then whiskey, and she was happy to find an unopened bottle of Coke in the fridge.

"I had them bring a few bottles of Coke for you."

"Thank you again." She joined him on the sofa. He said little at first, he just polished off his drink. He refilled his glass, and then he started in. They talked for over three hours. There were more tears, more yelling and more apologizing, but at the end of it all, Jacqueline had told him every detail, answered every last question and most of all, she told the truth.

"You sure you've told me everything?"

"Yes, I've told you everything."

"I want to forgive you once, Jacqueline. I can't hear something new next week, next month or next year. That would make me regret forgiving you."

"I totally understand, Legend, and I swear I've told you everything."

"Now, you need to call him and tell him that it's over, and tell him to stay away from you and to never dial or text you ever again," he said and handed her the phone. She dialed him as ordered. "Put him on speaker," he said, and she did. She told him everything Legend said to tell him and then ended the call.

"What now?" she asked.

"We take it one day at a time. I'm hurt and so disappointed in you woman, but I love you, and I forgive you," Legend said. He pulled his wife into his arms and prayed to God for strength because it would take a whole minute for him to heal after this.

Chapter Twenty-Four

Legacy

Legacy sat at her computer looking at the details of their bank statement. She noticed there were several charges for a Chinese restaurant that was near Tanya's house, and most of the dates were days when Kenny was supposed to be working late or out with the guys. She continued to scroll and saw a few purchases from baby stores, and her blood instantly began to boil. She snatched up her phone and dialed Kenny, but he let her call hit his voicemail. She didn't bother to leave a message, she sent him a text instead.

Where in the fuck r u

Legacy wat's wit u, who do u think u talkin 2

What's with u, when r u comin home we need 2 tlk

About what???

Come the fuck home n c

Just tell me Lay. What in the fuck is going on now!

Kenny just bring yo' lying ass home right the fuck now! I told u this Tanya bullshit ain't about 2 b no issue in this house. U can go back 2 her ass if u think 4 a min I'm about 2 be back on dat stupid shit wit yo' ass!

Legacy what is u talkin' bout

I'll c yo' lyin ass when u get home!!!

She was pissed. She took a closer look at the activity on their statement and knew Kenny wasn't eating all that bullshit from those restaurants because half the time he'd come home and eat like he hadn't had a morsel all damn day. Legacy printed out the statement and grabbed her highlighter. Anything that looked suspicious was now in pink, and she was putting Kenny's ass out if he was fucking around with Tanya's ass again. She was over being sloppy seconds, and she wasn't letting Kenny get away with shit.

About an hour later, he strolled into their condo like he was the king. Legacy muted the T.V. and tossed the remote. She got up and went over to the kitchen table and snatched the bank statement from the table.

"What is it, Lay? What are you so pissed about now? And I done told yo' ass about talking to me like that. I'm yo' man, not some damn kid," he said.

"And I done told yo' ass that I'm not going to have issues with you and yo' bitch ass baby momma, Kenny. Why the fuck is there charges for restaurants near that trick's house, Kenny? These are the days you text me with bullshit about working late. And you buying baby shit for that ho's baby when you don't even know if that kid is yours yet!" she snapped and then slapped him in the chest with the statements. He took it and did a quick once over.

"Babe, relax. You know Tanya was on bed rest for a whole minute, and there are times when I picked her up something to eat for her after work before coming home. Why in the fuck are you tripping, Lay? I'm not spending time with her, but when she was on bed rest I had to go by there and help her out, Legacy. And yes, I may have bought the baby a couple of things, Lay, what's the big deal?"

"Help her out with shit like what, Kenny? You're not her fucking man. She needs to call someone other than you, and it is not wise to be spending our hard earned money on a baby when you don't even know if it's yours!"

"Call on someone like who, Legacy, huh? And I'm starting to believe that I am the father," he tried to say.

But she cut him off. “What!” she yelled. “You don’t fucking know that for sure, Kenny,” she said, putting her hands on her hips.

“Wasn’t I here for you when you were on bed rest with Kennedy?”

“You were, but you knew Kennedy was your damn baby.”

“And what if this little boy is mine, and I don’t do shit to help her out? Then I will look and feel like an asshole.”

“Little boy? How long have you’ve known the sex of the baby?” A wave of agony rushed through Legacy’s body like she had been hit by a Mack truck. She knew how bad Kenny wanted a son, and now this bitch gets pregnant with his first son. It made her sad, and she wanted to cry.

“She told me today.”

“And when the fuck was you planning on telling me?” she spat. Her eyes welled, but she refused to cry over it.

“Legacy, language, damn. You are going to stop talking to me like that for real.”

She lowered her voice. “Again, Kenny, when were you planning on telling me?” she asked again. She turned her back to him to get the water from her eyes. She didn’t want him to see her cry.

“Tonight, when I got home, but I walked in the door to you blasting on me,” he said and moved close to her. He put his arms around her waist.

“Because I’m not finna let you play me, Kenny. I told you I wasn’t wit’ no drama with you and Tanya, and you promised me no secrets. You said we were good, and that you and Tanya was a done deal, Kenny. I don’t want you spending time with her at all. All you two have allegedly in common is a child together, and I won’t sit back and let you do me any ole kinda way. That shit ain’t gon’ happen ever again!” Legacy declared.

"Baby, come on, please don't do that. I am all in, and I'm not fucking around on you with her. I asked you to marry me, Legacy, and I won't ever fuck around with Tanya on you ever again."

Legacy pulled away. "Again? What in the fuck do you mean again, Kenny?"

"Baby, you know what I mean."

"No the fuck I don't! You cheated on me with Tanya before you moved out?"

"Legacy," he tried to say.

She stopped him. "No, Kenny! Did you? You told me that you and Tanya didn't hook up until after you and I broke up. You said you didn't get with Tanya until a few months after you moved out."

He let out a breath. "I lied, Legacy, okay baby, and I'm sorry. I started fucking with her when you were pregnant with Kennedy," he confessed.

"Son of a bitch! You had that bitch all up in my face like she was my friend when you were fucking her all along? You and that bitch are made for each other, and this bullshit I thought we had is just what it is, bullshit," she said and took off her ring.

"No, baby, please don't do this. You and I are good now. Legacy, you know I love you."

"Move, Kenny. I can't even stand to look at you right now."

"Come on, Legacy. That shit is in the past."

"Tanya was a friend, Kenny, a fucking friend. I thought that when I was pregnant with your damn daughter, and she was in my face so called helping while I was on bed rest that she was a friend, but her low-down gutter ass was sleeping with my man!"

"Legacy, wait. Stop. You constantly pointing the finger at other folks while you and I fucked around when I was with Tanya."

"Kenny, that was different!" she yelled.

"How the fuck so!" he yelled back. She opened her mouth, but nothing came out. "Yes, you don't have an explanation for that shit, do you? The bottom line is we've both done shit that was wrong, but we are where we are now because we're past the dumb shit. I swear on my son that I don't want Tanya. I want you, Legacy. I'm in love with you, and I'm sorry I lied. I'm sorry I ever got involved with her, and I'm sorry for all the times I hurt you. There is nothing going on with me and Tanya. We get along for the sake of this baby and if this kid isn't mine, I won't have another motherfucking word to say to her. She knows I'm with you. Baby, please put the ring back on. I'm begging you."

"I don't trust you, Kenny," she cried with her head down.

He lifted her head and kissed her forehead. "I know you don't, baby, but I'm doing all I can to show you that I'm for real. From now on, if you want to be with me every time I go to Tanya's, fine. I just want you to know that I won't fuck up this time. Baby, I love you," he said and gave her a few gentle kisses on her face. She slid the ring back onto her finger, and he kissed her deeply. Legacy was a big girl, but Kenny was a strong man, so he lifted her off the floor and put her on the kitchen table. He paused for a moment and took off his jacket and removed his shirt and tank. Legacy looked at her man standing there in his jeans and his shoulders, his chest and eight-pack abs looked as if it had been painted onto his skin by an artist.

He stepped out of his Timbs, undid his belt, button and zipper and let his jeans drop to the floor. When he rolled down his boxer briefs, he released his erection, and Legacy's nipples hardened and grew into the size of two grapes. Her gown hung off one shoulder, so Kenny pushed the fabric downward and exposed her left breast and nipple. He covered it with his mouth and sucked hungrily. Legacy had recently stopped breast feeding, but that didn't stop him from sucking her nipple hard like she liked him to. He pushed the other strap away and went for her other nipple, and Legacy gasped at the touch of his finger against her clit.

"I only want you, baby. You are all I need, and this pussy right here is the best pussy I've ever had in my life. I will never ever hurt you again, you gotta trust me," he whispered in her ear.

"Yes, Kenny, yes baby," she moaned. He licked two fingers and went back to her center. He teased her opening while he continued to please her nipples and then slid them inside of her.

"Ooohhh, babe, your pussy is so wet. It's already ready for me. You ready for me to fuck the shit outta you?" He pulled her body into his and pushed her legs back, holding on to her legs by the back of her knees. He let go with one hand and grabbed a hold of his dick and guided it in.

"Ahhh," Legacy moaned at the sensation his dick gave her upon entering her core. She loved having him inside of her, and she rested on her elbows on their kitchen table while Kenny fucked her right. He'd go slow, speed up and push himself all the way in to the hilt. Then he'd pull completely out, slap her clit with his rod and then glide right back on in. Kenny felt so good that Legacy called out his name over and over again. "Oh Kenny, Kenny, oh, Kenny baby, Kenny, it's so good," she cooed in between his powerful thrusts. He released one leg, and she grabbed a hold of it for him while he used his free hand to massage her clit. He pumped so hard and rubbed her clit so well, she squirted. Never had she ever squirted in her life. "What the fuck, Kenny! Oh fuck, Kenny, oh fuck, baby, oh fuck, fuck, fuck!" she bellowed.

"Ahhh yeah, baby, ahhhh yeah, ooohhh your pussy is so good, baby. I'm about to cum," Kenny growled and grabbed her right breast. He held on tight and then he grunted. "Oh shit, baby, there it is, oh fuck, there it is," he released. He stood over her and didn't pull out right away.

"Baby, did I squirt?"

"Yes, you did, and it was beautiful."

"How did I do that?"

"I don't know, but you did," he said and then eased out of her. They were both out of breath, but both smiling. He helped her down from the table and pulled her into his arms. "I love you, baby, and I'm all in."

"I know, Kenny, and I love you too." Kenny scooped up his clothes from the floor and then headed for the bedroom. Legacy went under the sink and grabbed the Clorox wipes and cleaned the table. She then checked the floor to make sure there were no drippings of their fluids. She turned off the T.V. and set their alarm. Kenny was already in bed when she went into the room. She climbed in the bed with him and lay in his arms. "Can I confess something to you, Kenny?"

"Yes, babe, you can tell me anything. After all the things I've done, whatever it is you can get a pass, except if you fucked Omari!"

"I know you didn't after what I learned about you and the whore Tanya earlier."

"Okay, okay, I'm joking. What's your confession?"

"I'm jealous that she is giving you a son," she said.

"Awww, baby, don't be. We can have more kids, and you know my girls are my world. I'm excited about having a son, but I was just as excited with Kierra and Kennedy."

"I'm sure, but I hate that she has a part of you, and we can't take it back."

"I know it's tough, Legacy, and I can only imagine how you feel, but you have all of me. If he's my son, I'm just going to be a good dad and try to get along with Tanya. I don't know how I can get you to see that you are the lucky one."

"I guess you're right, but no more secrets. Don't be going behind my back to do shit for her. I'm not playing. Even if you're going to take her Chinese food or change a light bulb or diaper when that baby comes, just tell me the truth."

"I promise I will," he said and then reached inside of her gown and went for her breast.

"Kenny, baby, what are you doing? We're having a conversation."

"And I'm listening while I play with your boobs."

"You are a mess."

"Yeah, you're right, and I'm about ready to make you squirt again."

"Oh no, Kenny, I'm tired."

"Just lay here and let me do all the work," he said, and she didn't fight him. She gave in and let him have her body until they were too exhausted to move. Sleep came easy for Legacy, and she rested easy in Kenny's arms as she fell into a deep night's sleep.

Chapter Twenty-Five

Mia

Mia headed home after another passionate night with Rene. She hated who she had become, but her flesh ruled, and she and Rene were fucking every other night. They had gone back to fucking in the office after hours, and she spent less time with Morris because she told him she was working late. Morris was still the sweetheart boyfriend who sent her flowers and unexpected lunch and spa treatments. Even though she and Morris had come to having sex once or twice a week, he still treated her like royalty, and she hated the ugly side of her that loved fucking Rene.

"Babe," Mia called out when she entered Morris' kitchen. The last few nights had been shared with her lover, so she for sure had to go to Morris that night after work. He made it clear that he didn't want to hear any excuses, and that he needed to see her. She hoped to walk in to Morris preparing something delicious, but the house was still, and Morris wasn't in the kitchen throwing down as usual. "Maybe he wants to go out for dinner," she mumbled to herself and went to the bottom of the steps and called out for him again. She was starving and wanted to know what type of plans he made for them for dinner. Within moments, he appeared and came jogging down the steps.

"Hey, you. I was hoping you were in the kitchen making something spectacular. Baby, I'm starving," she expressed. He gave her a nod and proceeded into the kitchen. He had a yellow manila envelope in his hand, but that didn't ring any bells. "Baby, hey. Can

I get a kiss, a hug or a salutation?" Mia asked. Something was off, but she didn't know what.

"Really, Miss Collins? You want to be addressed properly?" Morris said.

Mia was blown away, and her mind raced. "Miss Collins? Is this some kind of joke, Morris? You're addressing me so formally, why is that?"

"Have a seat," he said and gestured to the stool that she stood near.

"I'd rather stand. What is going on?" she inquired. Mia was no fool, and she could tell by his cold behavior that something was very fucking wrong.

"Well, Miss Collins, we are done. It seems you have a…What I wanna say…" He paused and put his hand on his chin like he was thinking of something clever to say. "A fetish for your ex-lover, Rene, so I am checking out of this bogus relationship."

"I'm sorry, come again? What are you talking about, Morris?" she asked nervously. How could he possibly know she had reconnected with Rene, and how on earth would he know they had been fucking? She was scared as hell, and she knew he could see the fear on her face.

"Oh, Miss Collins. Please, I beg you for fuck sake to not act naïve or pretend you don't know what this is. I told you that Victoria would be the last woman I allowed to cheat on me, and with that I put someone on you."

"You fucking spied on me!" she yelled. She wasn't mad that he scrutinized her, she was mad because she had gotten caught red-handed.

"More like tailed for a little while. You are just like her. You are a selfish bitch who doesn't deserve love. That man dogged you, dumped you like garbage and stayed with his wife. He and his wife double teamed yo' ass, and you still ran your ho' ass right back to him. Bottom line is, my dick was too small for you, not big as married fucking Rene's, and I didn't want to fuck you in your ass. I told you my deepest secrets about being molested and why anal was off limits, and you sat there and pretended like you cared. You

opened your lying ass mouth and told me you loved me, Mia, but you run back to him. Please fucking tell me why!" he demanded.

"I give you everything. I spoil you. I pamper you, and I fuck you to the best of my ability, but yet you run back to that sad ass married, no good ass motherfucker who will never leave his pregnant wife for your simple ass. You want to be a side-piece instead of a wife. You want to be this motherfucker's sloppy seconds, and you don't want to be nobody's wife. I fell in love with you and when you suddenly started working late and stopped wanting me to touch you as often, I got a feeling in my gut, and I was right. You want to be treated like a whore, Mia. You don't want to be loved, honored and cherished."

She sniffled. "No, that's not true. Please don't say that," she cried.

"Why the fuck not, it's the truth. If it were not, you would have never gone back to him. You are getting exactly what you deserve, Miss Collins, and as heartbroken as I am, I am ecstatic to tell your ass goodbye. Women like you don't deserve men like me. I'm not faithful because my dick ain't as big as Rene's. I'm a faithful because I have morals and values, and I loved your simple ass. I tried to trust you, I did, but you fucking changed. With each day you became more distant, so I hired someone to protect myself. You may think my actions were wrong, but I don't give a fuck. I do what I do to protect my heart from trifling bitches like you," he spat and then slid the envelope across the counter to her. "Oh, and another thing. The pictures in that envelope were already

FedEx'd to Mrs. Winters, now get the fuck out of my house!" Morris ordered.

He left the room leaving Mia standing there speechless and heartbroken. She loved Morris, but she was too caught up in her feelings over Rene. She didn't open the envelope because she already knew what she'd see, so she just turned to leave. She drove home in deep thought with mixed emotions.

A lot of what Morris said was spot on, but she was too busy trying to justify her actions to take what he said to heart. "He's just a jealous, little dick bastard!" Mia shrieked out loud, listening to her own words. She was dead wrong. It was her, not him. All he did was give her the best of everything, but she was so shallow and so full of herself that she did what the fuck she wanted to do, not thinking of the cost. When she got down to it, she didn't want Rene, she just wanted to please her flesh. Something her mother preached about constantly was not letting the flesh rule your spirit. Her parents had taught her better than that. She knew the values of marriage, love, honor and respect.

"Oh my God, what have I done? I just lost the best man you've ever sent to me. How could I be so fucking selfish and stupid?" she said out loud. "Oh, my God, please help me. I love him, and I have to get him back. I'm a stupid, self-absorbed idiot, and I allowed my desires for Rene to ruin my life," she cried. She made a U-turn and hurried back to his house. When she got there, she keyed in the code to the door lock and immediately knew it had been changed because it denied her access. She knocked for forty-five or so minutes, and he didn't answer. She sat on his porch and text and called, but still he didn't answer, nor did he reply. Mia paced his porch and sat out in the elements and continued to knock, but Morris refused to let her in. Defeated, she drove home. In tears, she prayed harder than she had ever prayed in her life. Her parents were God fearing, loving parents who taught her valuable lessons. Mia grew up with morals and values that she had packed away when she got involved with Rene.

"Lord, God, please hear my cry. Please answer my plea. I messed up so bad, Lord Jesus, and I may have lost the one you sent for me. If you sent him for me, please forgive me for my stupid lustful behavior and sins, and please put it on his heart to forgive me. I'm ready for love, God, and I know Morris is it, but I am horrible, and I hurt him. God, please fix it. In your son Jesus name, amen," she cried.

When she got home, she was surprised to see Laurie on her porch.

"What are you doing here, Mrs. Winters?"

"You know what the fuck I'm doing here, Mia. And if I wasn't pregnant with my third child, I would stomp a hole in your boney ass right here and now, but it wouldn't do any damn good."

"Listen, Laurie, I had a rough day, and I can't with you right now. Go take your frustrations out on Rene. He's the one who owes you an explanation, not me!" Mia hissed.

"Bitch, please. I didn't come here for you or to ask why. I don't give a rat's ass about you and stupid ass Rene. I just came to congratulate you."

"I'm sorry? I'm not following."

"Oh, but I am sure you are. I got the photos, so I know you and Rene are still fucking, but it's all good because I'm going to move out the way."

"Laurie, I don't want your husband."

"Hummm, that's a pity because I don't want his ass either. I originally came to congratulate you on your victory of taking a black woman's husband, but I see you're not in a celebratory mood, so I'll go and fill your lover in on the new rules. It was nice, Mia, and I would say I wish you well, but I wouldn't mean it, so why lie," she said and walked down the steps and to her car.

Mia couldn't process what just went down because her bladder was about to burst, so she hurried inside to use the bathroom. Once she was done, she started calling Morris again. That time she left a message pouring out her heart. "Everything you said about me is right, and I'm sorry. I was caught up on the wrong shit, and I'm so sorry, baby. I do love you, truly I do, but I'm flawed like a motherfucker, and I am begging you to give me another chance. Rene doesn't mean shit to me, and I don't want him like I want you. Please forgive me, Morris. Please give me another chance. I love you, baby," she tried to continue, but the voicemail cut her message short. She called back several times, and each time she begged him to take her back and to forgive her. Physically, she was attracted to Rene, but otherwise Morris had stolen her heart, and she'd do whatever it took to get him back and would never give up trying.

Chapter Twenty-Six

Anika

Michelle's smile faded, but that made NeNe smile even brighter. She knew Michelle was stunned to see her on Jaxson's arm, but Jaxson told her that the only way he was going to the funeral was with NeNe by his side. He wasn't doing anything wrong because he and Michelle were done, and NeNe hoped there would be no static that evening between them.

"JT, what a surprise. You didn't mention bringing a friend," Michelle said sarcastically.

"Well, Anika is my fiancé, and I thought it would be okay. If it's not, we can leave."

"Fiancé? I'm sorry, is that what you said?"

"Yes, you heard me right, Micky. Now, are you going to allow us to come in or do you want us to leave?"

"You are welcome to stay if you'd like, but you're not about to bring her up in here," Michelle roared, and a voice came from behind her.

"Is that you, JT? Come on up in here, boy," an older man said.

"Uncle Jessie," Jaxson said, and they basically moved Michelle out the way. NeNe's heart thumped as Jaxson pulled her with him inside of Michelle's family home. She hoped there weren't any big-boned sisters up in there waiting to jump her ass.

"Look who's here. My nephew!" Uncle Jessie announced, and everyone rushed over to greet Jaxson. Apparently, her family loved him. "Oh my, JT. You are still as handsome as ever. I don't know how my crazy ass sister let you get away," one woman said.

"I don't know, sis," Jaxson said and pulled me forward. "I'd like you to meet my fiancé, NeNe. NeNe, this is Madison, the coolest sister-in-law on the entire planet."

"Awww stop it, JT. You are such a charmer. Hello, NeNe, it's so nice to meet you," she extended her hand.

"You too," NeNe smiled. NeNe was blown away on how cool Michelle's family was. She could see why Jaxson loved them.

"Well, make yourself at home, and if you need anything just let me know," she told NeNe and was off. Jaxson introduced her to more people, and NeNe's neck was burning because she could feel Michelle's eyes on her. She felt a little uncomfortable initially, but everyone was so friendly she relaxed a little.

"Everyone is so nice, Jaxson. I was expecting to be blind folded and shot by the firing squad by now."

"NeNe, Michelle and I grew up together in the same neighborhood and went to the same school, so our families have known each other for years. They watched me and Michelle date off and on and other people, so nobody's bothered by me showing up with you. They are like my second family."

"Well, I'm sure Michelle doesn't share the same sentiments."

"Micky will come around. She's always been this way. She's always had this, 'I don't want you, but I don't want you with nobody else' and both of our families know it. If her mother were alive today, she would have greeted you the same welcoming way."

"So, do you think she'll stop gawking at me soon?"

"Most likely no, but don't worry about her. She's harmless, she won't make a scene in public or get too crazy around her family."

"I'm not worried. I just don't like the stares she's giving me."

"Stare back, see how it makes her feel?" Jaxson joked and laughed lightly.

"Honey, it's not funny," NeNe said and playfully hit his arm.

"Really, JT?" a voice interrupted, and NeNe knew that voice.

"Really, what? Micky, what do you mean?"

"Why would you bring her here? And why would you even want to be here, Miss NeNe? You strutting around my family's house like you're somebody fucking special," Michelle slurred. It was obvious she might have had one too many. "My family is grieving the loss of my mother, and you two are walking around like you're at a got'damn cookout!" she yelled. A couple of people looked their way.

"JT, let's just go," NeNe suggested and tugged his arm.

"Yes, just go!" Michelle yelled.

"Micky, why are you acting up?" Uncle Pete asked. "No one is bothered by this young lady being here with Jaxson, so go sit yo' ass down somewhere and stop acting up."

"Yeah, Micky, don't start," Madison added.

"Don't start? This is my got'damn husband up in my momma's house flaunting his new woman like he has no respect for me!"

"Michelle, stop it!" Jaxson said. "I didn't show up with NeNe to be messy, and if you had been here with another man I'd be fine with that. Our marriage has been over; we are just waiting on a final decree. If anyone other than you are bothered by me being here with NeNe, I'll gladly go, and you better not ever dial my number or text me ever again. Everybody here knows you, Micky, and everybody here knows that you do this every single time I'm with someone other than you. Since you've gotten everyone's attention, let's let everyone know what's really going on between us and why we are divorcing?"

"JT, you better not open your fucking mouth to tell our business!" she declared.

"No, Micky, this is how you want to play it, so let's do it," he threatened.

"Jaxson, baby, come on, don't," NeNe encouraged.

"No! They need to know why after all these years of us being on and off again, why our fairytale of a marriage has ended."

"Okay, JT, fine. I'll stop, just don't, please," Michelle cried. Whatever the secret was, she didn't want it to get out.

"Good, now please stop showing your ass. You know damn well I never do anything to deliberately hurt you, but you have hurt me over and over again, so can we have a little peace this evening without you doing this thing you do?"

"I said fine, JT!" she cried. Her eyes welled, and her hands shook. "I apologize, NeNe," she said and walked away. Her sister ran off behind her, and the rest of the family went back to having a good time. Jaxson and NeNe took a seat on the other side of the basement where the music wasn't as loud.

"I shouldn't have come."

"Nonsense. Everyone likes you."

"But this could have been worse."

"No, because I wouldn't put you in harm's way. If I didn't know these people like I do, I would have never showed up with you. I myself would have never even bothered to come. Michelle is not horrible. She just has some issues that she really needs to get help for because as long as I've tried, I couldn't help her."

"Do you trust me enough to tell me?"

"I will when we leave."

"Okay," NeNe said and didn't push the issue. They hung around for a little while longer. They played cards, danced and ate good and then said goodnight to everyone. Michelle wasn't anywhere in sight when they departed, and NeNe figured that was a good thing. When they got into the car, NeNe was anxious to hear the juice about Michelle, but she didn't ask. They talked about other things, but by the time they were settled in at her loft, she had to ask. "So, what's the big secret about Michelle?"

"It's been killing you to ask, hasn't it?" Jaxson smiled.

"Yes," she chuckled.

"Michelle has anger issues. She goes into these rages and fits, and she was physically abusive to me for a very long time. Over the years, it has gotten worse, but I dealt with it and tried to get her help, but she would never stick with the treatment. Since we were fifteen, we've been on and off and on and off. Maybe a year before we got married, she had it under control, no rages, no fits and no outbursts. Six months into our marriage, I had just gotten my realtor license, and me and a few of the fellas went to hangout. By the time I got home, which was later than I expected, she went into this rage and started throwing things at me and was yelling and literally foaming at the mouth. I had never seen her at that level of rage before.

"Anyway, I tried to leave, and she ran to block the door. At that time, I used to play softball on the weekends with my friends, and there was a bat propped up against the wall in the corner by the door. She grabbed that bat and started swinging at me, and that night she broke a couple of my ribs. You see this scar?" he pointed out. It was a tiny scar above his left eye. NeNe nodded. "I had to get five stitches. Over the years I dealt with it, but I just couldn't take that shit anymore, so the last time was the last time, and she doesn't want anyone to know that she use to go upside my head."

"Oh wow, I would have never suspected it."

"You've seen her work before."

"What do you mean?"

"When I'd say I got hurt on the court or weekend football with the fellas. Sometimes she'd just launch a glass at me. Living with her was difficult."

"You took me around that psycho? If she'd whip yo' ass, imagine what she'd do to me?" NeNe said, now feeling a bit uneasy.

"NeNe, she's never been that way with anyone other than me."

"That you know of."

"True, but I don't think you have anything to worry about."

"I hope not," NeNe said and then stood. "You want something from the kitchen?" she asked.

"A beer would be cool."

"One beer coming right up," NeNe said. She poured her glass of red, and they relaxed on the sofa watching T.V. until they dozed off.

Chapter Twenty-Seven

Reynard

House hunting had been a task, but he had finally found the one he wanted to make an offer on. He had no plans to buy a house in the beginning, but after working with his agent and going over the numbers, he could afford to buy a place, so that's what he did. It was a town house, something he was also dead set on not getting because he didn't want to share a wall, but he ended up getting an end lot, so he only had to share one wall. It wasn't the wall of his master bedroom, so it worked out perfectly. The unit was newly renovated with beautiful stainless steel appliances and had that glass back splash that NeNe always talked about adding to her kitchen at the loft, but they had never gotten around to doing it.

He still hadn't told Lisa a thing about moving, and he wanted to wait until his offer was accepted before he told her. His offer had gone in early that morning, and he impatiently waited six hours before his agent got back to him. He answered on the first ring when she called. "Hello," he said anxiously. It was like waiting on a million-dollar check for him.

"Reynard?"

"Yes, this is he."

"This is Camille," she said with a smile in her voice, and he knew that much because they had been working together for a little over a week.

"Yes, Camille, I know. Please tell me you have good news."

"I do. They accepted your offer. So congratulations, you've bought yourself a house."

"Are you for real? That is awesome. Thanks so much for everything you've done. I would not have found the perfect spot without you."

"You are more than welcome. Can you swing by my office so we can finalize the paperwork?"

"I can. In about an hour, is that good?"

"Sounds perfect, Reynard and again, congratulations."

"Thank you so much."

"You're welcome, bye now," she said and ended the call. Rey could have leaped for joy. He was so happy and proud of himself. He wanted to call NeNe, but he knew that would be a bad idea. He shut down his computer and headed over to finish up with his agent. On the way in, he saw her. She was looking so beautiful to him. Her skin was glowing, and her outfit looked sexy, yet professional. He wasn't going to, but he approached her. "Hey, NeNe," he said, and she turned to see it was him.

"Rey, what, what, what are you doing here?" she asked nervously.

"Relax, NeNe. I'm not here to cause any trouble. I'm here to see Camille. I bought a house," Rey announced.

NeNe didn't seem too enthusiastic at the news. "Congratulations," she said dryly and then turned to walk away.

He reached out for her arm. "Hold on, NeNe."

"What, Rey?"

"Listen, I know you hate me, and I know I'm the last person you want up in your face, but I must tell you how sorry I am for breaking your heart the way I did. I was living foul, and I truly am sorry."

She hesitated for a moment or two and then said, "You know what, Rey, I accept your apology."

"Thank you."

"No, thank you. Yes, you hurt me, but you made room in my life for a great man. I hate how things ended but I'm glad it did, so good luck with yo' man…I mean woman, and again, congratulations on the house," she said, holding up a folder, and he caught a glimpse at the rock she was wearing.

"Hold on, NeNe. Are you engaged?"

"I am."

"Hold the fuck on. We broke up two minutes ago, and you're getting married?"

"Indeed. The difference between grown ass men and boys is grown men know what they want and go get it. Boys play games with women like they are toys and when the toy gets old, they hunt for a new one. Grown men know when to put away childish things. That's why I'm engaged now because Jaxson knows what he wants. Not like you," she spat and tried to walk away again, but he stopped her.

"Look, I'm sorry I reacted that way. Everything you've said was right about me, and I am happy for you and wish you well."

"Thanks, Reynard. Same to you," NeNe said and then headed to her office.

"Oh, and tell Legacy I know it was her big mouth that told you," he yelled behind her but she kept walking. He shook his head and then headed to Camille's office. He sat thinking about NeNe, half listening to what Camille was saying and just kept signing where she told him to sign. When the paperwork was completed, he anticipated on closing in about thirty days. The unit was empty, so he didn't have to worry about a family being out on time, and he was anxious to move in.

"How about a drink to celebrate?" Camille asked.

"Sure, why not," he agreed.

"Let me grab my purse and coat. There is a pub not too far from here that I take my clients to celebrate."

"Cool," he said and went to wait for her in the lobby. They drove separate cars and once inside, they grabbed a booth. They exchanged small talk, ordered a little food and after a few drinks, they said their goodbyes. Camille promised she'd be in touch as the closing date approached and after thanking her again, Rey headed to Lisa's. When he got in, Joss told him that Lisa had just gone to lie down because he wasn't feeling well.

With that, Rey checked on him, showered and then headed downstairs to look through some of his stuff. He couldn't wait to get his things out of his basement and get back to enjoying his own space. Lisa was great and easy to live with, but if Joss was going to be there, he had to go. He went through a few boxes, and then he heard the door open from the first floor. He wondered if Lisa had gotten up, but within seconds Joss was at the bottom of the steps wearing a skimpy pair of boy shorts and a tank. She was braless, and Rey could see her erect nipples poking through the cotton.

"Do you need any help?" she asked.

"No, I'm good," Rey said, putting his eyes back on the task in front of him.

"I could sure use some," she said.

Not interested, but he asked anyway. "Help with what, Joss?"

"Well, I was wondering if you could help me to an orgasm. My pussy is so hot, and it hasn't been licked in a while, so if you could lick my clit, I'd be so grateful," she said so casually.

"Do you ever give up? I mean, we are in your cousin's home, and you're down here in my face again asking me to fuck. Do you know how stupid yo' ass look and sound right about now?" he spat. It was like she was a desperate fool, and that was such a turn off. "Do you know how many niggas there are in Chicago who would love to fuck yo' country ass, so why are you always coming at me? Go online, hit up

Tinder and find you some dick because I don't do thirsty ass bitches."

"That's because yo' punk ass is gay as fuck!" she snapped back. "Fuck you, you gay ass bitch!"

"Fuck you, you ho ass trick!"

"You gon' wish you had took this pussy when I offered it to you because when I tell Lisa you've been trying to fuck, she gon' put your sissy ass the fuck out!"

"You wouldn't dare go there, Joss. Don't even fucking lie like that," he pleaded.

"Fucking watch me!" she blasted and ran towards the steps with him right behind her ass. She ran into Lisa's room screaming and yelling, and Lisa was jolted out of his sleep. Rey stepped into the room right behind her.

"Baby, don't believe shit she says," he said, shaking his head. Rey wasn't the most perfect man on this planet, but he cared for Lisa and didn't want Lisa to think he'd stoop so low and try to fuck his cousin right under his nose.

"What the fuck is going on?" Lisa cried in a panic. Rey could see by they look on Lisa's face that the commotion scared the shit out of him.

"Yo' man just tried to get in my motherfucking panties, that's what!" Joss yelled.

"What?" Lisa said, brows vaulted.

"Baby, she is fucking lying. This bitch has been coming on to me since day one."

"You are a motherfucking liar, Reynard. It was yo' punk ass trying to smash, and I told yo' ass I ain't with dat!"

"You're fucking lying!" Rey yelled. The confusion and back and forth had Lisa yelling too.

"Fucking stop it, stop it, stop it you two. Damn!" Lisa yelled over them. All three of them were breathing hard. "You two are going to send me to the fucking ER with this shit!" Lisa said. "I am tired, I'm in pain and I don't have time to hear shit from you," he pointed to Rey. "Or you," he pointed at Joss.

"But baby, this ho is—," he tried to defend.

"I said fucking stop!" Lisa yelled. "It doesn't matter who did what, because if it was her all along, you didn't say shit. If it was him all along, your ass didn't say shit either," Lisa bellowed, pointing at Joss. "Both of you get the hell out of my house. Now!"

Both looked shocked to hear the words that came out of Lisa's mouth. "Baby, wait," Rey tried to plead.

"Reynard, if you say one mo' thing to me, I will get my ass up out of this bed and punch you in yo' mouth, and Joss you know me, so you betta use yo' feet and get the fuck on up outta here now!" Lisa screeched. Without words, they filed out of Lisa's room. Rey was floored and could not believe what had just happened. "Son of a bitch," he mumbled. He stopped in his tracks when he remembered all his shit was inside of Lisa's room. He went back and tapped on Lisa's door and then entered before he said come in. "Rey, I've asked you to leave, don't make me call the man on yo' ass."

"I'm going to leave, Lisa. I just have to grab some of my things."

"Yeah, you do that."

"Lisa, you just gon' sit here and not hear me out?"

"Hear fucking what, Rey?"

"My side," he said.

"Okay, what's your side, Reynard? Humor me?" Lisa chuckled.

"It was her, baby. She has been coming at me saying all kinds of dirty shit, and today she just flipped the fuck out. That bitch is lying because I wouldn't fuck with her ole country ass!" Rey voiced.

"And you know what, Rey, if I ask her the same thing, she's gonna tell me it was you and that you've been coming at her, so there. I am done with it. If she was living foul right here in my house under my nose trying to fuck, you should have told me from jump before she came barging into my room like she crazy as hell, so please go. I can't deal with either of you right now. I'm not supposed to be under any type of stress, and I've been through too much pain with my life changing experience to let either of you set me back."

"Just like that, you don't trust me."

"Rey, please just go."

He looked at Lisa and instantly became pissed off. After all he had done to NeNe for them to be together, he was just going to throw him out? "You know what, fine. What the fuck ever, Lisa. I was going to move out anyway!" he barked.

"Come again?"

"Yes, you heard me. I found a house, and I close in thirty days!"

"Oh fucking really!"

"Yep," he said and moved around the room to gather his things. He grabbed his duffle bag from the closet and put it on the chaise at the foot of Lisa's bed.

"So, when the fuck was yo' ass going to tell me you were house hunting and moving out, Reynard?"

"Well, I planned to tell you tonight when I got in, but you were sleeping, and I didn't want to wake you."

"You know what, fine. For you to even decide to house hunt without me lets me know where we stand."

"Are you serious right now? I was doing that for me. I got tired of you saying how this is your damn house, Lisa. No man wants to hear that shit."

"You know what, you're probably right, and if your ass was paying all the motherfucking bills then you could say what the fuck you want."

"Lisa, don't even fucking go there. I contribute to this house. Don't sit there like I don't give you shit."

"That funky ass five-hundred dollars you give me a month ain't shit," Lisa said.

"Oh wow," Rey said. "If that was the way you felt you should have opened your mouth and said something. I had no problem with giving you more. You don't have a house payment or a fucking car note because your father left you a trust, so I didn't think you were strapped. But it's cool, we're done anyway." Rey continued to pack, and Lisa sat in his bed in tears. He didn't know if what Lisa said was out of anger because he thought he was trying to smash his cousin, or if he truly felt that way. Either way, Reynard was leaving. "I'll be back in a few days for the rest of my shit," he said. Lisa said nothing. Rey figured that was the man in him because no woman had ever allowed him to leave so easy.

When he got outside, stupid ass Joss was loading her car. She looked at him. "Don't say a motherfucking word to me," he said.

"I'm sorry," she attempted.

"Bitch, whatever!" Rey said and tossed his shit in the back seat. He got in his SUV and peeled off. He called up a friend of his from the gym, and he had a place to crash until he closed on his place. Even though he and Lisa were over, Lisa was nice enough to let his things stay at his place until he closed so he wouldn't have to move his things twice. That he was truly thankful for. After that day, they texted and talked a couple of times about the incident, but somehow Rey couldn't get Lisa to understand the reasons why he didn't come to him first, when Joss made a move on him. Lisa said he could no longer trust him and decided that it was best for them not to get back together. Rey agreed, because if Lisa thought he'd do something like that to him, with his cousin, being apart was a better option.

When he returned to pack up his truck, he thought things would be odd between him and Lisa but they weren't and he was happy to see that Lisa recovered well. He still wondered how his new pussy would have felt, but he knew damn well that that wasn't going to happen, not after all the hell Joss raised when her country ass was in Chicago. After he gave Lisa a final hug, he got into his U-Haul and then deleted Lisa's number from his phone. "Time to move the fuck on," he told himself with a bright smile on his face.

Chapter Twenty-Eight

Omari

Victoria's due date was approaching fast, and Omari was doing everything he could to prepare for his son's arrival. Her family had planned a huge baby shower for her, and he was excited that it was co-ed. He and Victoria decided they would be together and give the relationship thing a shot since they were having a baby together. Something about her being pregnant and a mixture of her pussy being so damn good persuaded his decision, but he didn't regret it. He wasn't completely over his crush on Legacy, but they grew to be good friends. When he introduced Victoria to Legacy, they hit it off well, and things were going fine for them so far.

"Where do you want the gift table to go, Auntie Val?" Omari asked Victoria's aunt. The shower was scheduled to start at five that evening, so Victoria was at Sassy Styles where Legacy worked getting her hair and make-up done for her special event.

"Over there near the table where we're going to put the cake," she said.

"Yes, ma'am," Omari said and quickly moved in that direction. He wanted everything to be perfect for Victoria and after the last couple of months he had shared with her, he was happier than he had ever been in his life. He and Victoria had worked together on the baby's nursery as far as the design and décor. He did all the painting, shelf hanging and assembling, and Victoria just told him where to put what. He couldn't wait to meet his son.

"So, what I heard about you and Victoria is right?" a voice interrupted, and Omari turned to see Morris standing a few feet away.

"What the hell are you doing here, Morris, and why?"

"I came to chat with my ex-wife. Is she here?"

"Vicky is at an appointment."

"What type of appointment? She stopped taking my calls months ago. She's not living with her grandmother anymore, and she even changed doctors on me."

"Not that it's any of your business, but we're together now, and we are going to raise our son together. She stopped taking your calls and texts because when you told me to go see about my kid's mother, I did. She doesn't need you anymore. I got her medical coverage, so no she's not going to that broke down ass clinic anymore."

"Oh, so you stepping up, taking responsibility for your child I see?"

"If that's what you want to call it, yes. Remember, you told her that bastard baby ain't yours, and you disposed of her."

"That's so like you. Picking up another man's trash."

"Who happens to be my treasure, so tell me why you're really here?"

"I'm here because I need to talk to Vicki. I've given it a lot of thought and even though I despise you and can't stand the sight of her cheating ass, if this kid is mine I have to do the right thing. I heard through some friends that her shower was going to be here today, so I was hoping I could speak with her and let her know that I'd be willing to be tested and if this kid is mine, I want to be a part of his or her life."

"Well, Morris, you wasted a trip coming down here because according to our calculations, you are not my son's father, and there will be no DNA testing. No one is testing our kid."

"Do you hear how stupid your ass sounds right now, Omari? Now that you are back in that good pussy, your judgment is clouded. I don't give a damn if you don't want to test that little boy, but I do, because if he is my son he will know me, and I will have joint custody of him. You can be his step-daddy if you'd like, but if he is a Vallinas, he will have my name, and I will be a part of his life."

"Since when did you care about Vicky or this baby? You didn't hesitate to throw her on the streets with only the clothes on her back while possibly pregnant with your kid, and now that you're feeling bad you want to stake a claim on my son!" Omari roared. He wanted to grab Morris by the neck and squeeze the life out of his ass.

"That whore cheated on me. What was I supposed to do, throw a party? Give her another chance? You fucked my wife all over my got'damn house, Omari. What kinda friend does that to a man he calls brother? And not once did your sorry ass ever say you were sorry for having my wife, *my wife*!" Morris yelled, pointing at his own chest. Victoria's aunt and two cousins quickly vacated the room.

"Morris, I know what I did to you was low, and you are right, I never told you that I was sorry for touching your wife. I was dead wrong, but I just wanted to be there for her. She was so sad and lonely while you were chasing the money, and she used to just cry on my shoulder time and time again because you wouldn't slow down or even bother to take her on one damn trip with you. I just wanted to make her feel wanted, and I fucked up man, I screwed up big time. One thing about doing the wrong thing is you never stop to think about how wrong it is until you get caught doing it. And I'm sorry."

Morris didn't speak right away, he paused before he spoke. "I wasn't the best husband, and at the time I was working my ass off to secure a future for my wife and whatever children that God may have blessed us with. I forgive you, Omari, but we can never go back to being friends. I didn't come here to cause any problems for Victoria. I just want to know the truth about this baby. If it's mine, I want to be there. I want to be a better father than my father was to me. You have known me since we were in college, and you know the hell I suffered when that teacher did that shit to me and my father did nothing!

I confided in you because I thought you were my brother. The abuse and the things that happened to me, I'd never let anything like that happen to my son, so don't deny me my rights to my kid. If he's not mine, I'll be out of your hair, and you two can live happily ever after, but if it is my child, I want to be a father," Morris said. They both stared each other down for a few moments, and then Morris turned to walk away.

"I'll talk to Victoria this evening after the baby shower," Omari called out after him.

"Please do," Morris said and walked out the door.

Omari stood in one spot for a few moments before he could move. He was so confident and sure about the baby before, but now Morris had put a hint of doubt in his mind, and he hoped the outcome would not be in Morris' favor because he was ready to be a dad and wanted the baby to be his.

Chapter Twenty-Nine

Legacy

Legacy listened to Victoria go on and on about how sweet and kind Omari was treating her. She told her more details than Legacy cared to hear, but she listened because she knew how it felt to be newly in love. She remembered that feeling with Kenny, and she was feeling those feelings again because since the night of their last argument, Kenny had been extra sweet, extra attentive and she never once had to wonder where he was because as promised, he kept her in the loop. Kenny was working overtime for her and Tanya to become cordial again, and Legacy knew that shit would never happen because she despised that bitch and didn't want to make peace with her at all.

"So, are you excited about the shower?" Legacy asked as she cut Victoria's hair into layers.

"Am I? I can't wait to see what they've put together for me. Omari was so secretive. He wouldn't even let me look into any of the bags, so I can't wait."

"I bet. I had a shower with my first baby, but not with my second. I was on bed rest for a long time during my second pregnancy, and they ended up taking her by C-section, so I never got to do a shower. My girls kept trying to plan one, but that bed rest made it difficult, and then my girls said they'd have one after Kennedy was born, but folks just got too busy."

"I know that all too well. I know you know the history of me, Omari and my ex-husband, Morris, but to be honest, if he would have just slowed down a minute and just breathed. Morris was the type of man who never stopped to smell the roses, and I was so lonely. I hated I slept with Omari. I could have gone elsewhere looking for comfort, but my stupid ass went for my husband's best friend of all people. I regret everything except for conceiving this baby. I was terrified at first, didn't know what in the hell I was going to do because I knew this baby wasn't my husband's, and Omari straight bailed on me, cut me off and refused to even acknowledge me, but you turned him around when you encouraged him to talk to me. So thanks, girl. I owe you big time."

"Child, hush. You don't owe me a thing. Love and relationships are the hardest things to deal with for people. Our feelings always get us hurt or make us do the unthinkable. When you're in your feelings, all you see is what matters to your heart and most times, you're not rational. Your feelings can make you settle for things you ordinarily wouldn't settle for, and your feelings most times keep you stuck on stupid, but what I've learned in my years on this planet is that there is nothing wrong with being in your feelings when the person you're with is in their feelings too."

"Girl, you are so damn right, and when a woman finds a man who is in his feelings for her, she better act right because only one out of ten men get in their feelings, the rest of them ain't worth shit," Victoria said, and they laughed.

"You are so right, Victoria," Legacy added and then a familiar face walked through the door. "Mia," Legacy said, noting her girl looked a damn mess.

"Lay, what the hell? I've been calling you and NeNe. Are y'all just too damn busy for your friend?"

Legacy had seen a couple of missed calls from Mia, but she kept forgetting to call her back. "I'm sorry, baby, but I have been a little busy. What's wrong?"

"It's over. He found out and put me out and now he won't talk to me!" Mia cried.

Legacy took a quick pause. "Hold on, Victoria. Can you give me a minute?" Legacy asked.

"Sure," Victoria said.

"Come to the back and tell me what in the hell is going on," Legacy said, and Mia followed. She had on yoga pants, an oversized hoody and her weave was up in the messiest bun Legacy had ever witnessed on Mia. She couldn't remember the last time she had seen Mia without make-up and when Mia removed her shades, her eyes were red and swollen. "Mia baby, what is going on with you? What happened?"

"Morris found out that I started back fucking with Rene," she cried.

That was new news to Legacy because she had no idea Mia was sleeping with the enemy again. "What the fuck! When did you start back fucking with him, Mia? What in the fuck is wrong with you?"

"I know, Lay. Damn, please, I feel horrible enough. I was wrong on so, so many levels, and I'm so fucking sorry, and Morris won't talk to me, and Legacy, I love him so much, and I don't know how to get him back, please tell me what to do. He is the best man I've ever met in my life, and I fucked up bad, Lay. I fucked up, and I lost him," Mia sobbed.

Legacy had to get back to her client, and she didn't have a quick answer. "Listen, I'm going to call NeNe, and we can get together tonight and see if we can figure out something together. I'm sorry you are going through this, but you know this is what happens when you fucking cheat."

"I know, Lay, and I'm so fucking sorry. I can't eat, I can't sleep and I just need him back and don't know what to do. Morris is my—," she was trying to say, but someone interrupted.

"I'm sorry, Legacy, but Omari just called and said he has to pick me up a little earlier than three. Can you tell me what time I'll be done?" Victoria asked.

"I'll be right there, Victoria," she said. "Listen, Mia, I gotta get back to work. This girl is having her baby shower today, and I have to finish her up."

"I understand, but please will you and NeNe come by this evening, please?"

"We will, I promise," she agreed. Mia put her shades back on, and Legacy walked her to the door. She hugged her tightly. "I'm sorry, Mia."

Mia nodded and left. Legacy hurried back to her station. "I'm so sorry, Victoria, but I'll have you done as quickly as I can."

"I don't mean to pry, but that's your friend Mia, right?"

"Yes, her name is Mia."

"I think she is dating my ex."

"Oh my fucking word. How did this shit go over my head? She told us months ago about Morris' ex-wife messing around with his best friend and got pregnant. This is so freaking unbelievable. Why does someone involved in my friends' situations somehow always end up in my chair?"

"What do you mean?" she asked. Legacy continued to work her magic on Victoria's hair as she filled her in about Lisa and Rey.

"I swear, no one can make this shit up. It's crazy!" Legacy said.

"It is, and I feel bad for your friend. Morris is not the forgiving type, and I can tell you now I doubt if he takes her back."

"I understand. It's sad, but I can't say Mia was right for what she did."

"Neither was I, but we all make mistakes. We're only human and when you love someone, not saying they should get a free pass, but you should at least try to show some mercy."

"Well, I'm with a repeat offender, so you are preaching to the choir. If I didn't love Kenneth Green as much I do, that brother would have been chopped," Legacy joked.

"Well, just pray for me and Omari. I don't think I can take another love loss."

"I will, and I wish you two the best."

Chapter Thirty

Legend

It had been a few months since Lake Geneva, and things were still not back to normal. Legend and Jackie were doing well, but he still hadn't touched her. She'd tried to entice him, but he was not interested. He just couldn't get the image of her being bent over that desk out of his head, and he was having a difficult time letting it go. They cuddled, talked more than they've talked in a very long time and went back to date nights and making time for each other, yet he still couldn't make love to her.

"Legend, I think we should see someone," Jackie suggested. They were having dinner alone. The twins were at a friend's house, and the baby girl was at Legacy and Kenny's for the night.

"See someone for what?"

"For our issues. You have forgiven me, and God knows I'm grateful for that and the time we've been spending together is beautiful. I love our text filled days, and I love that we are becoming close again, but I miss you, Legend, and I need you to touch me. Baby, I want our intimacy back. I want you to make love to me," she sniveled. Her eyes were heavily glossed with tears.

"I'm just not ready, Jackie, and I don't think a doctor can make me ready to have sex with you again."

"Baby, we have to try something. I know my affair was five minutes ago, and I know I can't put a time limit on your healing process, but I need you back. I need you back in my bed. You stay up all night on the sofa watching television to avoid lying next to me and when you do come to bed, it's so late that you lay on top of the covers with your clothes on. I know I hurt you, and it kills me every time I think of what I did to you, but I need you back in my bed. You are my husband, and I need you to touch me, Legend."

He took a sip of his wine and focused on his plate. He couldn't look at her. "I'm not ready to make love to you, Jackie. That image of him fucking you from behind…" he paused. His eyes burned, but he refused to hold back his tears. "It still haunts my mind, and sometimes when I look at you I get so fucking angry and question my decision. Like, like, like was it the right decision to stay? Do you still think of him, do you want him to fuck you again? Was I terrible in bed? Was his dick better than mine? Did he do you better?" he confessed. His face was drenched and when he looked at her, so was hers.

"I'm sorry, Legend. If there was another word or something else I could do to show you how sorry I am, I'd say or do it in a heartbeat, but there is nothing I can do but wait patiently for you to come back to me. It's my fault, so I will wait, and if you don't want to go to counseling, okay," she said gently. She stood and put her cloth napkin on the table. She walked by him and went to their bedroom. Legend didn't follow her because he felt they both needed space.

His appetite had escaped him, so he got up and cleared the table. He loaded the dishwasher after putting away the leftover food. He went downstairs to his man cave, clicked on the television and as he scrolled through the channels, he landed on the local news. He left it there and gave the television some volume.

"A woman was killed today in a car crash on HWY 290 on her way home from work. Investigators are not yet sure what caused the woman's vehicle to lose control, but police are saying that it's a possibility the woman hydroplaned. The woman was thirty-eight and leaves behind her husband and three children. Up next, the crisis with school vending machines," the anchorman said. Legend muted the television after hearing that. His heart skipped because he thought about Jackie. What if it had been his wife who lost her life that day, how would he feel? If she was gone from his life forever, how would he cope?

He turned off the tube and raced up the steps and took quick strides to his bedroom. He walked in, and Jackie wasn't in their room. He heard the shower going, so he went in to join her in the shower. When he opened the door, he was shocked to see his wife sitting on the frame of the tub with one leg up, opened wide, and pleasuring herself with a vibrator.

Startled, she quickly stopped and put her leg down. "Oh my God, Legend, you scared me. I'm so embarrassed," she said, getting up and fumbling to turn off her toy.

"No, baby, don't stop. I want to watch you."

"Huh?" The look she wore on her face was of confusion.

"You heard me. Go back over and sit back on the side of the tub, lift your leg again, spread your pussy wide open for me and play with your clit with your little friend."

She hesitated. "Legend, are you sure that's what you want?"

He undressed staring her down. "Yes, I want to watch you play with your pussy and after you cum, I want you to deep throat my dick and swallow my nut the way I like it," he groaned. Before he was down to nothing, she was in position doing exactly what he told her to do. Legend stroked his dick as he watched his sexy ass wife satisfy herself with a little pink device that was no larger than his dick when he was twelve. The way Jackie moaned, he knew that little pink motherfucker had some power because her facial expressions and moans told him that her gadget was getting the job done.

Too anxious to wait until she climaxed, Legend walked over to her and rubbed his dick over her lips, and she instantly opened wide for him. He groaned as he allowed his wife access to his body, something he thought wouldn't happen again for a very long time. "Yes, baby, yes that's it, suck that dick, baby. That shit is good, you are making me want to cum, baby," he grunted. "Yasss, yasss, yasssss," he growled. It had been too long since he bust one, and he was ready within moments to let it go. Jackie moaned louder and squirmed, and he knew that meant she was there. When her eyes looked up and locked with his, it was over. Nut shot out of him like a bullet from its chamber.

Jackie didn't stop bobbing her head until he pulled away. "My God, baby, that was so good. Baby, I missed you so much, come here," he said, reaching out for her, and she got up and walked into his arms. "I love you, Jackie, and everyday I'm going to show you how much I do. I didn't mean to punish you, but the thought of not having you in my life is something I can't imagine."

"I love you too. I'll never leave you, Legend, and I'll never hurt you ever again." He believed his wife, and that night he made love to his wife over and over again. The next morning was the same and that night a repeat. They vowed they would never tire of pleasing each other, and he knew their words were true.

Chapter Thirty-One

Victoria

The shower was lovely, and Victoria got way more gifts than she imagined. There were people who showed up for her that stopped talking to her nine months ago after the fiasco with Morris, but they had accepted that she did something wrong to him and not them. Before the evening came to an end, Omari surprised her with the best gift of all, an engagement ring, and he begged her to marry him before the baby was born. Of course, she agreed.

Later that night after Omari got all the gifts unloaded, he joined Victoria on the sofa. "How are you feeling, my love?" he asked.

"My lower back is aching, but other than that I feel good. Today was like one of the best days of my life, and I am so happy," she smiled brightly. "And my ring is beautiful. I did not expect this. I mean, I have to ask you though," her tone got serious.

"Ask me what?"

"Are you absolutely sure you are marrying me for me? For Victoria, and not because of my baby? If you marry me, Omari, and for any damn reason at all this is Morris' baby, will you still want to be with me?" she asked. Her eyes brimmed with water, but she had to know the truth.

"Listen, Vic, don't cry, baby, please. The day I approached you on the porch at your grandma's, I'd say there is no way in hell I'd married this woman, not even if she was carrying quintuplets by me, but each day after I grew fonder of you, then I started liking you, and then I started loving you. I have no fancy answer or fancy words to soothe your ears. This is me, an old ordinary hard working guy. I don't have a mini-mansion like Morris, and I can't drape you in Prada, Gucci and Louis, but what I will do is keep a smile on your face daily. I will be a good husband to you and do my best to be a great dad to our son.

"Even if by chance our calculations were wrong, and Morris is the biological father of this kid, he will still be ours, and I will love him just as much as I love you."

"Awww, baby," Victoria said and leaned in to hug him. And as soon as she made that move, her water broke. "What the fuck, Omari. My water just broke," she said in a panic.

"Oh shit!" he said when he looked down at her crotch. "Are you for real right now?"

"I think it is," she said, trying to stay calm. "All right, help me up so can take off these wet pants," she said, and Omari stood. He reached out both hands and then pulled her up from the sofa. "Now, baby, pull my pants and panties down," she instructed. He did exactly what she said, and she stepped out of them. "There should be a black and white striped skirt on the chair in my room, get it please." Victoria was calm because she had felt no contractions, but her lower back was throbbing like a son of a bitch. She held on to Omari's shoulders and stepped into the skirt. "My bag is already ready in the nursery. Grab it and the diaper bag because it's game time," she smiled. Omari kissed her lips and then dashed to get the bags. The ride didn't take long, and only in a little discomfort, labor was treating her well.

They got her in and examined her, and she was at four centimeters dilated. They offered her drugs, but she declined because her lower back was the only thing that was nagging her. The monitor said she was having a contraction, but she swore she didn't feel it. Her labor progressed slowly, so she agreed on something to help her rest and take the edge off her back pain.

"Baby, I have something I need to tell you," Omari said softly.

"Please don't tell me no bad news, Omari. This is supposed to be the best day for us, remember?"

"And it is, but I must tell you that Morris came to the reception hall today when you were getting your hair done. He wants the DNA test."

"Why are you just now telling me, baby?"

"Because I wanted you to enjoy your day and not have any stress on your plate."

Groggy, she yawned. "I don't care, Omari. He can have it. I just want to meet my baby boy and love him and take care of him. I want you to be the father, but if chances are you aren't, I just want to be happy and raise my kid." A tear fell.

"Don't worry, baby. This is the best day of our lives. No matter what happens, we are in this together."

"Do you promise?"

"I promise."

"Well, do me a favor and let Morris know I'm in labor. There is something I need to talk to him about anyway."

"Something like what, babe?"

"Can I tell you later, I just want to sleep now," she said with her eyes fluttering.

"Yes, baby. You rest, and I'll go call Morris."

"Ummm-hmmm," she barely nodded, but she felt Omari kiss her face. A few hours later, the pain woke her out of her sleep. "Omari?" she called, but he didn't budge. "Omari, baby," she said louder, and he jerked from his sleep.

"Yes, baby, yes, I'm up. What is it?"

"Baby, please get the nurse. I'm in a lot of pain," she said.

"Okay, okay," he said and hurried out the room. Within seconds, he and the nurse came back in. Victoria was in a lot of pain, and she knew it had to be time because she wanted scream. The nurse talked to her in a soothing voice as she checked her, but Victoria wanted to cuss. Even the nurse touching her hurt.

"Well, you are at seven, so we should have a baby here soon. I'm going to page your doctor."

Victoria nodded. She gripped the bed rails and heard Omari talking, but all she heard was "blah, blah, blah, blah, blah," because she was focused on the pain. Thirty minutes later, she was wailing in pain and kept yelling she wanted to push, but the nurse insisted she not push.

"Listen, lady, I don't know what the fuck to do to stop this feeling, and I need to push got'dammit!" she yelled. The nursed took a look.

"Well, this baby is coming sooner than we expected. Hold tight for a minute," she said and left the room. Not even two minutes later, Victoria's doctor walked in ready.

"Hey there, Victoria. It looks like you are about to meet your son," he smiled.

"It looks like it, doc. Please hurry because I really need to push," Victoria panted. The doctor took his position and then pushed her legs back.

"Son, you hold this leg while the nurse holds this one. The baby is right here, and he is ready to make his entrance. Now, give me a big push, Victoria," the doctor said. She gave it all she had, and she was so disappointed that one push wasn't enough. "You are doing a great job, and the head is just about out, so give me another big one like you are having a BM, now push." Again, she gave it all she had and still had to push four more times before he made his way into the world at 5:31 a.m. Victoria was out of breath, and her body trembled uncontrollably, but she had done it. She had given birth to her first baby. When the nurse put him in her arms, she didn't need a test to tell her shit. He was Omari's. He had Omari's nose and lips, but her eyes.

"He's your son," she cried tears of joy. "He's ours, Omari. He's our son," she sobbed. She was so relieved and so happy. Omari went to the nursery with the baby while they cleaned her up. What seemed like an eternity but was less than two hours, Omari and their baby were back in her room. When her son latched onto her breast for the first time, she had no idea that it would sting so bad, but she welcomed the pain. "All right, little O, I'm so happy to meet you," she said.

"You're giving him my name?" Omari asked.

"Yes, of course."

"They say looks on a baby mean nothing, but I can see me in him, Victoria, and he is beautiful. Thank you," he cried. She had never seen him cry before, but she understood why. He rested his face against hers, and they both fawned over their new bundle until Victoria could no longer keep her lids open. Omari put the baby in the bassinet and then Victoria heard clicking sounds.

"Omari, what are you doing, baby?"

"Taking pictures. I have to post my son on my Facebook, and then I'll get some z's."

"Be sure to tag me."

"I got you, baby," he said.

Later that afternoon, Omari went out to get them something to eat, and Legacy sat up in her bed cradling her newborn. He looked more like Omari the more she stared down into his little face, and she thanked God for answering her prayers. If Morris would have been her child's father, she'd get plenty of financial support and was sure he'd be a good father, but she wanted nothing to do with him.

There was a tap on the door. "Come in," Victoria sang, not taking her eyes off her new bundle of joy. The scent of his cologne, Mont Blanc, hit her nose, and she didn't even have to look up to know who it was. "Hello, Morris."

"Hello, Victoria, and congratulations."

She looked up at him. He was still handsome as could be in his Hugo Boss trench and leather gloves. He looked like a million bucks as usual. “Thank you. I’m guessing you’re here for a sample of my son’s DNA?”

“Yes, I am. I don’t want to take up a lot of your time, I just want to get this over and done.”

“I’m fine with that, but do you want to take a look at him first? He is a splitting image of his father, and that’s not you.”

“Well, Victoria, not like you, I don’t give a damn about looks. I want to make sure that your son is or isn’t my son.”

“I’m fine with that, Morris. Let’s get it done.” Morris removed his coat and gloves and laid them on a nearby chair. He stepped out of the door and shortly after a nurse came in with him and got samples from Morris and the baby. Victoria had no dispute because she wanted it over and done just as bad as he did.

“Thanks, and until the results come back, is there anything you need for the baby? I will give you anything you need because if he turns out to be mine, I want to know that I’ve taken care of him from day one.”

“We are good. Omari has taken care of everything.”

Morris paused and then asked. “Can I hold him?”

Victoria looked at him strangely. “Are you sure you want to do that?”

“Yes, I’m positive. I’ve anticipated this day too, Victoria.”

She hesitated, but handed her baby to him.

“He is beautiful, and I know you think he favor’s Omari, but I don’t think so. He looks just like you.” Victoria didn’t argue. With a man like Morris it was pointless. “Happy birthday, little man, happy birthday,” Morris said and let the baby hold on to his finger. The image of him holding her son was sweet, but not as precious as the image of Omari holding him. "He is a beautiful baby. If you need anything, no matter what it is, just say the word."

"Thanks, Morris," she said. He handed the baby back to her and took one last glance at him.

"Would it be too much to ask if I wanted a picture of him?"

Victoria wanted to say hell no, but she nodded yes. He pulled his phone from his pocket, and Victoria allowed him to snap a couple of pictures. "Thanks. I won't brag or show off the pictures until I know for sure," he said.

"Of course," she replied. He went for his coat, and she stopped him. "Can I talk to you briefly about something else before you leave?"

"Sure, what about?"

"Your girlfriend, Mia," Victoria said.

Morris' eyes widened. "Mia, how do you know Mia?"

"I don't know her personally, but I know of her through a mutual friend, and I saw her yesterday."

"Where?"

"At her best friend's salon when I was getting my hair done yesterday. She came by there, Morris, and she was in pretty bad shape."

"And!"

"Listen, Morris. I was your wife, and I know you. I know how well put together you are and how you go by the book. You run a very tight ship, but Morris, we are not all like you. We are all cut from a different cloth. You act as if you've never heard of the word forgiveness. We don't all dance to beat of the same drum, and we fuck up. You may have been perfect your entire adult life, but us normal folks fuck up every now and then. I know cheating is a horrible thing to do to someone, but sometimes we are just so damn selfish that we don't stop and think that what we've done can or may destroy the other person."

"Make your point," he said with his jaws tightened. She could tell he was already losing patience.

"If you love her, don't throw her away or under the bus like you did me. Love her beyond her mistake. She was a girlfriend who cheated, not like me, your wife, so go to her and give her another chance. She loves you. If you'd seen how she looked, you'd know it. To come out in public looking destroyed as she did, she is hurting, Morris. For once, give someone you love a second chance," Victoria said tenderly.

Morris just nodded, put on his coat and hurried out of her room. She had no clue if she had gotten through to him, but she hoped for Mia's sake she did. She had overhead her and Legacy's conversation and being the two-timer that she had been, she felt her pain. People do dumb shit and make bad choices, and to forgive someone you love at least once is honorable, not stupidity she thought and then she smiled at her blessing in her arms.

Chapter Thirty-Two

Kenny

Kenny, Legacy and the girls were at Beggars pizza for dinner, and Kenny recognized a familiar face. He didn't want to interrupt, but she was just the person he wanted to see since he hadn't been to an appointment with Tanya in months. "Hold on, baby, that's Dr. Crawshaw," Kenny said.

"Who is Dr. Crawshaw?" Legacy asked.

"She's Tanya's doctor. Let me go over and speak."

"Okay," Legacy said.

Kenny made his way over to her table. "Dr. Crawshaw, how nice to see you?"

"Hello," she said and looked up at Kenny. From the way she examined his face, he could tell she didn't recognize him.

"I'm Kenny Green. I'm LaTanya Simpson's baby father, remember me? I was with her on a few of her visits earlier on."

"Of course, yes, I remember you. How are you and LaTanya? I am so terribly sorry for your loss. LaTanya was devastated, how is she doing? Are you two trying to conceive again?"

"Excuse me?"

"You and LaTanya, are you two ready to try for another baby?"

"I'm sorry, Dr. Crawshaw, maybe you're mixing me up with a different patient. LaTanya is due to deliver in about three weeks or less."

The look on the doctor's face was incredulous. "I'm sorry, Kenny, but the only LaTanya Simpson I know of that came into my office with you is no longer my patient since the incident occurred. I haven't seen or spoken to her since her follow-up appointment, and that was months ago. I'm sorry, but by you being the father, I was sure you knew."

Kenny's ears rang, and his vision blurred. He knew she didn't just tell him that Tanya had lost the baby when he felt her stomach and watched her body change. She had even told him that she was having a boy. "I'm sorry, Dr. Crawshaw, and I didn't mean to interrupt your dinner. Thank you for your time." He walked away and didn't look back. Kenny's heart raced, and he feared he'd collapse. What in the fuck was happening to him? He'd never thought he'd be in a situation like that one.

"Baby, what's wrong? You looked terrified," Legacy said. Kenny was speechless. "Kenny, what's wrong, what did her doctor say? Is everything okay with the baby?"

"Call Legend and see can him and Jackie look after the girls."

"Baby, what is it?"

"Just do it, Legacy!" he yelled and stood. He ran out of the restaurant because he needed some air. It was February, one of the coldest months in Chicago, but Kenny was so numb he felt nothing. He punched the air a few times mumbling obscenities and before long he was crying. He was beyond upset, and going to see Tanya that night was a very bad idea because he'd choke the life out of her body.

He took deep breaths and waited until he could hold a straight face before he headed back inside. As soon as he got to their table, he kissed and hugged his girls tightly and then leaned in to hug Legacy. He was so emotional he couldn't hold back the tears, and he sobbed in Legacy's neck. She just said, "whatever it is, we will get through together, it's all right." He heard her words and knew they had to get out of the restaurant. He grabbed a napkin and wiped his face while Legacy put the baby's coat on.

"Daddy, what's wrong?" Kierra asked.

"Daddy's fine, baby. Put your coat on so we can go to uncle Legend's," Legacy said. "Baby, just go get the car, I'll settle up the bill and bring the girls." He grabbed his coat from the back of the chair and before he vacated the building, he stopped by the doctor's table again.

"Thanks doctor, you have been a great help." He then hurried out and pulled the car up to the door. When Legacy walked out with the girls, he got out and took the baby and put her in the car seat and reminded Kierra to buckle up. They got in, and he was grateful that Legacy didn't ask any questions. She just held his hand. They took the girls over to Legend's, and then Kenny told Legacy everything the doctor had said. Legacy was hotter than fish grease. "Ooohhh, dat ass is mine. Kenny, please don't try to stop the beat down, because I'm going in."

"I won't stop you, but she has to confess first and once she does, do what you gotta do," Kenny said and they rode to Tanya's house. Her vehicle wasn't there, and Kenny was more than disappointed that she wasn't home. He pulled out his cell and called her, but his call went straight to voicemail. He and Legacy sat in her drive way until after midnight, but Tanya never showed. They decided to call it a night and revisit her ass the next day.

That night, Kenny couldn't sleep, and he tossed and turned.

"Baby?" Legacy said.

"Yes?

"Tell me what are you most upset about?"

"What do you mean, Lay?"

"Are you mad because there is no baby, or are you mad at the lies and deceit?"

"Do you want me to be honest?"

"Please do."

"Both," he said.

"Why is that?"

He turned to her. "As a man, it's like a badge of honor to impregnate a woman. I'm not saying I was super thrilled about the mother, but I was excited about being a dad all over again. The deceit is a totally different level of anger, and I don't understand why she didn't just tell me that night. She has been walking around with something under her clothes, Lay. I mean, it felt real. She took her betrayal to a level of mind games and after I confront her tomorrow, she is dead to me. To do that to a person is lower than a corpse rotting in a grave, and I can't see ever speaking to her again."

"I don't want to sound insensitive, Kenny, but I'm relieved, and if you want a son, we can try for another baby," Legacy said.

"Didn't you say no more after Kennedy?"

"I did, but we are a family and if you want another baby, let's make another baby." He pulled her close and kissed her. As angry as he was, he still made love to his woman.

The next day, he and Legacy got up and headed to Tanya's salon. She was going to be exposed that day.

Chapter Thirty-Three

LaTanya

Her due date was approaching super-fast, and Tanya was on edge every second of the day. She was short tempered and couldn't relax without swallowing a bottle of wine and a couple of sleeping pills every night. Kenny's visits became shorter and farther apart and instead of them growing closer, they were drifting further apart. He and Legacy had set a wedding date, and the only conversation Kenny had for her was strictly about the baby, and Tanya felt as if she'd lose her mind. *Oh, Lord what am I going to do? This baby is supposed to come in less than three weeks, and I don't know how to tell him. Do I fake a miscarriage today?* At this point, he'd want to see a baby, even if it didn't survive. Tanya's mind was in overload, and she had no clue what to do next. She thought about leaving town, but where on earth would she go? She couldn't stay away forever.

She owned a home and a business, and she was still pushing her hair products, so running wasn't an option. She let out a deep breath and went back to the front to get started with work. It was cold as ice outside, but that never deterred black women from getting their hair done, so she stretched before going back to her booth. The fake baby bump had weight on it, and she had the largest size it came in strapped on, and it was a heavy load to carry. She went to the front desk to see who her first client was. It was a shampoo and style, and she knew that client would be a breeze. Clients started to walk in, and she and her staff got to work. By one o'clock, the salon was packed. Tanya needed a break, but she kept right on working.

In the mirror, she saw that Kenny had come in, and she couldn't hold back her smile. It was always good to see him, and she was happy with his surprise visit. Mostly all her staff and clients knew Kenny and would often make chatter about how sexy he was, so she loved when he came in. He approached her station. "Hey you, what brings you by?" she asked gleefully.

"I was on this side of town, so I dropped in to check on you and the baby. How you feeling? How is my little man in there?"

"Well, I'm sure he's chilling in there while I'm tired, out of breath and going to the bathroom every five minutes. I'm so ready to have this boy so I can get my body back."

"Don't worry, it won't be too much longer. Before you know it, he'll be here," Kenny smiled. He looked good as usual, but something was a little off.

"Everything okay with you? You look a little, I don't know, melancholy. Is things good with you?" she asked, concerned. Kenny was always upbeat and cheery.

"I'm good, just thinking about the baby that's all and since the due date is approaching so fast, I'm a little anxious and nervous."

"Well, so am I. I have never had a baby before, and the women up in here keep telling me how bad it hurts, so you got it easy. Hell, I'm terrified, Kenny."

"I know. I just can't wait."

"And I can't wait neither," she said. She wished her words held some truth to them, but her motto now was, lie until you can't lie no more.

"I bet, because you look like you about to burst," he said, reaching in to touch her belly.

"Kenny, gon' now before I burn my client. You can't be feeling all on me in front of company," she playfully shoved him. She had a client in her chair, and she never cared for him touching her fake belly much.

"All right, all right, I'll let you get back to doing you. I'll see you later," he said and gave her a quick kiss on the cheek and then walked out.

"Girl, if your son look anything like his daddy, you gonna have to barricade your door when he becomes a teen."

"I know right. He is sexy and good at everything in and outside of the bedroom," Tanya teased, and they chuckled. She continued to style her client's hair while they chatted. About ten minutes later, Kenny walked back in, and she thought that was strange, but she hit him with her smile. It wasn't anything wrong with a double dose of him.

"Hey, what's up, Kenny? Did you forget something?"

"I did," he said, and then a second later, Legacy walked in behind him.

"Kenny, what is she doing here? You know I don't want her up in here," Tanya said with a tone of irritation.

"I know, I know, but we don't intend to stay long," Kenny said sharply, and his jaws tightened. He had a look on his face that Tanya recognized. That was a look of anger, and something had pissed him off.

Tanya became nervous, and fear overtook her body. She put the curling wand down because she was literally shaking. "What in the hell is going on, Kenny? What is this about?" she asked nervously. Her heart pounded hard in her chest, and she felt like she was about to be jumped.

"We are here to get the truth, Tanya," Legacy spoke up.

"I need y'all to get up outta here. This is my place of business. Kenny, whatever issues we got we can talk about them, but not here. I'm begging you." She was terrified, and she knew that somehow, he knew.

"Naw, LaTanya, it's not going to work like that," Kenny chuckled.

Her eyes welled. "Please, let's go into my office. I will talk to you, I will tell you everything. Please, Kenny, I'm begging you, not out here in front of my clients and staff," she pleaded softly.

"No, bitch, things ain't going down like that. You are an evil ass liar," Legacy said between clenched teeth.

Tanya was shaking uncontrollably, so she moved towards her office, hoping they would follow. "In my office, please. We can talk there," she said.

Legacy and Kenny took a couple of steps and then Legacy said, "No, un-un, fuck this. I don't owe you shit but an ass whippin, so this is where it's going down!" Legacy shouted.

Tanya turn back to see that they were posted in the middle of her salon, and sheer panic took over her entire body. She just stood there and let it happen because there wasn't a damn thing she could do but defend her lie. They couldn't prove it. No way would either of them put their hands on her in front of so many witnesses.

Everybody, listen up!" Legacy shouted. Stylists and clients ceased banter and gave their attention to her. "My name is Legacy, and this here is my fiancé, Kenny. We are here today to confront this miserable bitch who I once called my friend for faking her pregnancy," Legacy let it be known.

Tanya's heart sank when she heard the room gasp and the whispering start.

"Legacy, get out of my salon please and just leave me alone. Kenny, you don't have to be a part of my baby's life. I get it, you don't want this," Tanya continued to lie. She had to turn it around. "Just leave and I will never contact you again. Just don't do this to me like this. Please, just leave and I will stay away," she sobbed even harder.

"Bitch, you still gon' fucking stand here and lie?" Legacy said.

Tanya kept her eyes on Kenny, not Legacy. She was pleading with her eyes for him to have mercy on her and to pull Legacy up out of there, but that miracle didn't happen. He and Legacy were tag teaming her ass, and she had no ammo to return fire.

"Lift up your shirt, Tanya," Kenny ordered.

"What, no, no, no, no, I will not do that, Kenny. Please, I'm begging you to leave. I told you I will never contact you again, just please stop this." Tanya felt like she was having a heart attack by how rapidly her heart was beating against her chest. She didn't want to be exposed like that, and she somehow had to stop it from happening.

"Lift up your got'damn shirt now!" Kenny roared, walking up to her.

"No, and you need to leave now!" Tanya ordered with a firm and direct tone, pointing to the door. Her entire body was quivering, and she had to escape, so she turned and tried again to walk away, but Kenny grabbed her arm. He held on tightly and dragged her back to the center of the room. Eyes were wide open looking at them, and Tanya thought she'd die at any moment. She wished someone would do something to help her, like force them out, but everyone just stared at them. Everyone wanted to see the outcome of that performance, but Tanya still didn't buckle.

"You are a fucking liar. You have been lying to me for months about carrying a baby that died. Now, you are going to lift up your damn shirt and show me your stomach. If there is a baby inside of your stomach like you fucking say, lift up your motherfucking shirt!" Kenny's voice thundered.

All Tanya could do was beg. "Kenny, please I'm sorry, I'm sorry. Please don't do this to me, I'm sorry. I wanted to tell you. I swear to God, I tried to tell you so many times, but I was afraid to tell you. Just go please, stop this!" she wailed.

"Please believe how sorry I am," she continued to weep. Everyone stood frozen, watching the scene like it was scripted. Kenny didn't release the grip on her arm even though she tried to fall to the floor. Kenny snatched her top up over her tummy, and there it was for everyone to see.

Tanya was so humiliated, she wished she had passed out. Everyone started flashing pictures, and the whispers grew louder. Kenny released her arm with a push.

"You stay the fuck away from me and my family, understand? I never want to see your conniving ass face ever again. If you ever come near us, I will choke the living shit out of you. Do you hear me? What you did was unforgivable, and if you had told me the truth, I would have grieved with you and no way would I have turned my back on you. Now, stay the fuck away from me!" he spat in her face.

Tanya stood defeated in the middle of the floor and just sniveled. Kenny walked over to Legacy and took her by the hand, and they walked out. Finally, after all the drama, a few of her stylists rushed over to comfort her, but she didn't want anyone to touch her. "No, no, no! Please don't touch me, just don't fucking touch me!" she screeched.

She walked slowly to her office, shut the door and then locked it. She slid down the wall and cried harder than she did the day she lost her baby. The truth was finally out, but why did he choose to do it so publically in front of everyone? Tanya knew she'd be the butt of every joke for a very long time and just wanted to disappear. She didn't want to face anyone.

She stayed in her office for hours. Every time someone knocked on her door, she yelled for them to go away. She couldn't show her face, she had just been exposed for telling the biggest lie a woman can tell to a man, and she knew it would take a long time before people would ever stop talking about it. She got up from the floor and took off her top and removed the fake belly. She looked it and wondered what in the fuck was wrong with her to go to that extreme? How did she lose herself like that? Was her jealously for Legacy that severe? Now that it was over, she started thinking rationally. Where in the hell would she have found a baby? What would she have done when it was time to deliver?

"You are one twisted bitch," she said to herself and flopped down on the sofa. The tears were like a faucet, so she just let them fall. She stopped thinking about it. It was done, and now she would try to move on with her life. It wasn't like she had murdered someone. She just faked a pregnancy. "No, you didn't murder anyone, but what you did was stupid as fuck!" she scolded herself. "I'm just so glad it's over. I didn't lose him because I never had him. His heart has always belonged to her," she said. She laid her head back and listened to all the laughs and banter on the other side of her office. They were talking about her ass, just like they had talked about her stylist, Carmen, when she hid in the closet at her man's house because his wife came home early from a business trip. Just like they talked about her client, Sandra, for getting caught having sex with one of the deacons in the pastor's office. So many had been talked about, laughed at and joked on for the stupid shit they had done, and just like them, it was her turn.

It was well after midnight before she unlocked her office door. The shop was quiet as a mouse, and she was positive everyone had gone home. She walked over to her station and found it cleaned with a note on the mirror.

Hey Boss,

Sorry things went down like that today. We took care of your clients for you and don't let this get you down. Some of us have done worse. We all still love you!

Tanya snatched the note down and balled it up. She appreciated what her staff had done for her, but she knew they would be shaking their damn heads at her for a whole minute. She had taken it too far, now she had to live with the embarrassment. She opened the drawer to her station, and her phone was dead. She was afraid to even charge it and power it on. She knew the news had spread, so she figured she'd face the world the next day and not get a glimpse of it that night.

She went back to her office for her purse and keys, and that silicone tummy was on the couch. She grabbed it and stuffed it into her oversized purse and headed home. When she got home, she felt safe and wished she could just stay there alone until everyone had forgotten about what she had done. She plugged her phone in, but she still didn't power it on. She dragged herself to the shower and then after she went back down for a glass of wine. She stood at the counter and after a few trickles of wine went down her throat, she felt more relaxed.

She then thought it wasn't as bad as it seemed. She could handle a few laughs because what she had done was truly bogus. She grabbed her glass and the bottle and headed up to her room. If she could get through the next few weeks of cracks and jokes, she'd survive.

Chapter Thirty-Four

Anika

After the funeral, NeNe wanted to head home but Jaxson begged her to go to the repast because a lot of his family members would be there. Since he couldn't introduce her to many people at the funeral, the repast would give her an opportunity to meet some of his folks. She had already met his step-mom and dad. That's who she sat with because Michelle acted as if she needed Jaxson by her side so bad, so he sat with her and her family in the front. NeNe despised Michelle, but she had patience and knew Michelle would be completely out of their hair soon enough.

NeNe was glad she met more of Jaxson's relatives because every five minutes he was being pulled in so many directions, and if she hadn't gotten acquainted with anyone, she'd be ready to leave his ass there and go the fuck home. "NeNe, right?" a voice asked, and NeNe looked up.

"Yes, I am NeNe."

"Hi, I'm Jenna, Jaxson's baby sister," she introduced.

NeNe stood to hug her. "Hi, I've heard so much about you, and you are just as beautiful as your brother described you."

"Thank you, so are you," she said, and they took a seat. "I didn't make it to the funeral and barely made it here because my car broke down, but thank God I finally made it."

"Indeed, I'm happy you made it. How did you know who I was?" NeNe inquired.

"Oh, JT gave me a point in this direction. Crazy ass Michelle got him running all over the damn place like he is still her damn husband."

"I'm glad that came out of your mouth and not mine. I don't want him to know that she irritates the hell out of me."

"Well, she irritates the fuck out me," Jenna said. Shocked, NeNe gave her a surprising look. "Don't look at me like that. You know that bitch can tap dance on a nerve."

"Jenna, you are the most perfect sister-in-law thus far," NeNe chuckled and took a sip of her lemonade.

"Girl, I'm just glad I'm getting a new sister-in-law because that bitch right there," she said, nodding in Michelle's direction. "Is crazy," Jenna said.

NeNe didn't know if she knew what went on with Jaxson and Michelle, so she just said, "From what I've seen, she is."

"And you ain't seen the half," Jenna said and went into her purse. She pulled out a shot bottle size of Grey Goose. "NeNe, please pass me that pitcher of lemonade so I can fix myself a drink."

NeNe grabbed the pitcher and sat it near Jenna. She cracked opened the shot, poured it into the plastic cup and then added a little lemonade. "Damn, Jenna, I need one of those."

She dug into her purse again. "Here you go, sis. I can't be around my family and Michelle's family at the same time without a little something-something. And since we family now, if you want more after this, we can take a little walk to my car. My parents don't drink, so when I visit Chicago I have to keep my stash in my luggage," she laughed.

"So, why don't you come stay with us? I'm sure Jaxson won't mind."

"You are different from that evil bitch. Welcome to the family, big sis," Jenna said. She and NeNe were stuck together for the rest of the evening talking about people and laughing like they've known each other for years.

"I'm going to run to the ladies room," NeNe said.

"Okay, I'm going to go see if there is any more of that fried chicken left."

"Ooohhh, if so get me a piece."

"I gotcha," she said. NeNe hurried to the bathroom because the liquor was working its way through her, and she had to go bad. She squatted and damn near moaned because it felt so good to relieve herself. She heard the toilet flush in the other stall, but continued to do her business. When she was done and stepped out of the stall, Michelle was at the sink freshening up her face. NeNe kept her eyes on the faucet as she washed her hands and didn't even look at Michelle.

"So, you think you've won?" Michelle asked.

Confused, NeNe replied, "Won what, Michelle?"

"Jaxson."

NeNe laughed and shook her head and then snatched a couple of paper towels from the dispenser. "I don't think anything, Michelle. There is no competition between you and me." NeNe had a couple in her and had an "S" on her chest, and if Michelle wanted some, she would give her some.

"Oh there is, and you don't know how dirty I can play. You don't know the history between JT and me, so enjoy him as long as you can because he always finds his way back to me."

"I'm not worried about that happening, Michelle. You don't know me, and you don't know how dirty I can play. You think you can intimidate me, well you're wrong. You got away with putting your hands on Jaxson because he's a gentleman and for some reason he used to love your crazy ass, but now he's with me, and I know how to take care of my man."

"Bitch, you don't want to see me," Michelle threatened. "There is a side of me that you never want to see," she said between clenched teeth.

NeNe wanted to laugh in her face. Michelle was all bark and no bite, because if she truly wanted to rumble, there would have been fewer words exchanged.

"Oh, I see your horns. You are standing here like a raging bull wanting to attack. I can see that in your eyes because crazy recognize crazy. That look, that tone and that little foaming thing you got going on at the mouth right now may have ran off the others, but let me tell you something, bitch. I don't scare easily, and I don't run. I'd rather get my ass beat to the white meat than to back down like a coward ass bitch. So, if you think you want to pounce on me or go head to head with me, try it, and I will slay your motherfucking ass!" NeNe said in her face. NeNe was nobody's bitch, and she knew it was more of the liquor talking than she, but Michelle had infuriated her so much she wanted that ho to swing.

Michelle just stood there breathing hard, not saying shit. NeNe knew she wasn't tough. She only bullied Jaxson because she was safe with him. Jaxson wasn't the type to strike a woman, even in self-defense. NeNe grew tired of the stare down, so she stepped back and picked up her purse from the sink. She turned to Michelle and gave her one last up and down. "I thought so, you scary ass ho," NeNe spat and walked out of the bathroom. She couldn't wait to tell Jenna the details of what had happened in the bathroom. She had Jenna rolling and after that, Michelle didn't look her way. A few minutes later, Jaxson finally sat down and joined them.

"Where my drink at, sis?" Jaxson asked.

"How you know I got something?"

"Come on now, sis. You and NeNe over here giggling and shit, you got something."

"I do, let me run to my car. I'll be right back," Jenna said and stood.

"Baby, are you almost ready to go?" NeNe asked.

"Yea. When my sister gets back we can head out."

"Jenna is coming to stay with us tonight."

"What, Jenna coming to stay at my house? Y'all must have really hit it off. She'd never stay at my house when I was with Micky."

"Well, Micky is not a nice person. And that bitch tried to punk me in the bathroom."

"What, what happened?" Jaxson asked. NeNe gave him the details, and they both laughed their asses off. "Not big and bad Michelle."

"Yes, that bitch looked like she wished she had a trap door to fall into," NeNe said between laughs, and Jenna came back.

"What's so funny?" Jenna asked.

"Yo' girl tried to run up on NeNe in the bathroom," Jaxson laughed.

"Oh shit, NeNe told me. Man, I wish I could have recorded that shit," Jenna laughed with them. They continued to laugh about it, and then they decided to leave. Jenna said she'd meet them because she had to run to the bathroom before leaving. Jaxson and NeNe said goodbye to a few people on their way to the door and before they could make their exit, Michelle called out JT's name.

"Not a-fucking-gain," NeNe mumbled.

"Be nice," Jaxson whispered and squeezed her hand. "What is it, Micky? We were leaving."

"I know, and I wanted to say thank you for all your help. Losing my mom was hard, so thank you for still being here for me and my family even though I know I didn't deserve it." Her eyes welled. "I just wanted to tell you I'm sorry for all the pain and anguish I caused."

"No, Micky that isn't necessary—,"

She cut him off. "No, JT, please allow me to finish. Okay, this is hard for me as it is."

"Go on," he said.

"I put you through hell for many, many years, and you put up with me and took me back and then took me back again. I've meddled in your relationships and ran women off, and I am sorry. I won't do anything else to prolong the divorce. I will be by one day this week to empty out the garage, and I wish you two well," she said and wiped her eyes.

"Thank you, Micky. I know that was extremely hard for you to say, so thank you."

"Oh, and here," she said and stretched out her hand. "Your key."

"Oh, you can keep it. I already changed the locks," Jaxson said.

"Aw'righty then. Goodnight," she said.

"Goodnight," both NeNe and Jackson said in unison.

"Baby, please pinch me because I have to be dreaming," he said.

She pulled his arm so they could walk out the door. "Nope, you are wide awake, and I guess your past girlfriends were straight punks," NeNe joked.

"No doubt, but you are my hero, and you saved me from the diabolical Michelle."

"Well, I do what I can," NeNe joked, and they headed home.

Chapter Thirty-Five

Mia

After a few days of crying her eyes out, it was time to return to work. She had taken four sick days, and she didn't want to exhaust all of her paid time off, so she got herself together as best as she could to return to work. She stepped off the elevator on her floor and made a pit stop in the break room. She topped off her coffee that she had gotten from McDonald's that morning, replaced the lid and then snatched one of the glazed donuts from the boxes on the counter. She bounced to her office, greeting her co-workers with good mornings and hellos. When she stopped at her door, she noticed that her name plate was no longer in the metal brackets attached to the door. She found that to be odd, but she walked into her office and was taken off guard by her boss, Mr. Murray, and his assistant, Claudette.

"Good morning." Her eyes scanned the room, and she saw that all of her personals were no longer where she had left them, and the spaces on the wall where her degree and awards hung were all gone.

"Good morning, Miss Collins," Mr. Murray said.

"Hi, Mia, and good morning," Claudette spoke without looking directly at Mia.

"What's going on? Are we moving or renovating, or am I getting a bigger office?" Mia asked. She felt uneasy and wondered what in the fuck transpired while she was out.

"No, we're not. Have a seat," Mr. Murray said with a hand gesture towards the chairs that sat in front of Mia's desk.

"I'd rather stand," Mia said. She wanted to toss the donut and coffee because she felt the news she was about to receive would make her want to throw it at his ass.

"Fine, if that's what you'd like."

"I would," she snapped. "Just tell me what this is, Keith," she said, not addressing him formally as he had addressed her. He never called her Miss Collins any other day, why would he start that day?

"Well, this wasn't an easy decision, believe me, but we have to terminate you."

"What!" Mia snarled in disbelief. Her ears had to be playing an evil trick on her because she just knew she wasn't being terminated. "On what grounds? I've never had one tardy or one unexcused absence in the entire time I have been here! My reputation with this company is impeccable. What is this about, Keith?" she asked, raising her voice. She was angry and confused as fuck.

"Claudette, could you give us a moment?"

"Yes, Claudette, we need a moment," Mia shot her. She and Claudette weren't best friends, far from it, but she could have given Mia a heads up. A simple text would have worked. They had hung out together outside of the office on numerous occasions, so why didn't she give her some type of warning, Mia wondered as Claudette hurried to vacate the room.

"Mia, please have a seat," he insisted.

Mia didn't want to sit, but she went over and tossed that donut into the damn trash. She took her purse from her shoulder, dropped it into the empty chair near her and then sat her coffee cup on the desk. "I don't want to sit, I want answers. I'm the best on this team. My campaigns are better than any other employee on this team, so why am I suddenly being let go?" She crossed her arms over her breasts awaiting his explanation.

"It is because of your inappropriate behavior with Rene Winters." Mia's mouth dropped opened. She then took a seat. She wondered how he knew. "We received some photographs of you and Rene in some pretty obscene positions in this office, Mia, and that is unacceptable. I didn't want to release you, but that code of conduct is not tolerated here. And to do what you two did in your offices was out of line, Miss Collins, and frowned upon."

Mia heard him talking, but it sounded like gibberish because her brain wasn't processing his words. She wondered how Morris could go so far to ruin her career. Their business was personal, but he'd get her fired? It didn't add up.

"Keith, if I may, who sent those photos?"

"Mia, I umm…I'm not at liberty to share—," he tried to say.

She cut off his words. "Please, Keith," Mia pleaded. Her eyes brimmed with tears. She hoped Morris didn't hate her that much to send them the pictures. Whoever he had hired was top notch. She wondered why she and Rene never thought to close their office blinds. Even in their hotel room they barely shut the curtains, so that allowed Morris' spy more provocative pictures than just them leaving the hotel lobby or kissing in the parking lot before their final goodbyes.

"I wish I could, but policies are policies, and we're not supposed to break the rules."

Mia wanted to punch his white ass in the face and ask him how many times he had cheated on his wife. There were rumors about his old perverted ass too, but all Mia did was stand up and take the news like a grown woman. She'd gotten caught, and she was sure Keith enjoyed looking at those photos of her and Rene. She eyed the open box on the desk and knew it was her personal items. She grabbed her purse, slipped the strap over her shoulder and grabbed her box.

"Oh, Mia, one last thing. We need your badge," he said. She rolled her eyes. She wished his ugly ass would have told her that before she picked up the box. *Idiot,* she thought to herself and then put the box back on the desk. She went into her purse and retrieved her badge and handed it over. She grabbed her box and headed for the door. "Good luck, Mia. You will be missed and if ever you need a referral, reach out to me. I'd be happy to say good things."

"Thanks, Keith," she said and headed out. It didn't take away any of the pain she felt in her stomach, but at least he offered. She headed to the parking lot, and the tears ran down her cheeks. She had never been fired from a job in her life, not even at the White Castles on 110th and Halsted when her drawer came up short forty-four bucks. Her boss didn't send her packing. What in the hell was she going to do next? She had worked her ass off at the company and didn't want to have to learn the ins and outs of another brand. She knew Wyndham hotels and starting over made her feel defeated. She had come so far, but Rene was the source of her misery. He was the reason she'd lost her man, and now her job.

After loading her box of personals into her trunk, she got into her car and just sat there. "God, I know I've done so much wrong, and I'm getting exactly what I deserve, just please God, have some mercy on me and let me find another job quickly, and please stop my heart from aching for Morris," she prayed and then cranked her engine. She wanted to hate him for sending those pictures to her job, but she couldn't because she loved him too much. If he had done what she did to him, she might have done the same old dirty shit. She pulled out her phone and dialed NeNe.

"Hey, girl," NeNe sang.

"Hey, can you conference in Lay? I'm driving, and I can't be fumbling with this damn phone."

"Cool, what's going on?"

"The things I have to say I don't want to say twice, NeNe, so please get her on and then I'll tell you."

"Okay, hold on," she said. A few seconds later, she was back on. "Ok, Mia," NeNe said.

"I'm on."

"Legacy," NeNe called out.

"Yea, I'm here, what's up?"

"Well, Mia needed us both, so go ahead, Mia, spill it."

"I got fired."

"What!" they both shouted in unison.

"Yes, they let me go."

"What the fuck for?" Legacy asked.

"Can y'all believe he sent them damn pictures to my boss?"

"Nooooo!" NeNe cried.

"Yes, girl, and I need a girl's night. Can y'all please come by after work? I need wine, Mary J and you two to tell me that it's not as horrible as it really is," Mia cried. She didn't want to, but she became upset all over again.

"Awww, Mia. Don't cry, sweetie. Of course we will come by," NeNe said.

"Yes, as soon as I leave work I'll be over."

"Thanks," she sobbed. "Shit just went from bad to worse," she sniffled.

"Don't worry, Mia. If you need anything, we got you," Legacy added.

"Thanks, just come and bring a bottle or two, I have to drink away my sorrows."

"We got you, boo," NeNe said. They ended the call and something was nagging Mia to go to Morris and cuss him the fuck out. How could he be so damn evil to get her fired from work? How could he hate her so bad when he claimed he loved her? To fuck with her finances was lower than the affair, so she headed to his office. She had to confront him and ask him how could he do that to her.

She parked and hurried inside. She marched to his office and walked right by his assistant who tried to stop her, but Mia proceeded. "Ma'am, you can't go—," she called after her, but Mia had already barged into his office. There were three other men sitting in his office, but she was so livid she didn't care.

"How could you do that to me, Morris!" she demanded.

He looked up from his papers to see the intrusion. "I'm sorry, sir. I tried to stop her," his assistant quickly explained.

"It's okay, Rosa," he said and waved a hand. She turned to leave.

"Mia, what is this? Why are you barging into my office behaving like a lunatic?"

"You think I'm crazy, Morris? I can fucking show you crazy for what you did to me."

"What I've done to you?" he chuckled. "Mia, I advise you to leave my office now before I call security," he warned.

"Oh, so now you're going to have me arrested, Morris? What else do you want to do to get back at me, huh? You dumped me, I get it Morris. I cheated, and you kicked my ass right out, but to send those photos to my job, Morris? How could you do that to me!" she yelled. Tears began to fall. "I lost my fucking job today!" she spat and held up her arms at her side. "You sent those pictures to my employer, and I lost my fucking job! Are you happy now? Are we fucking even? Does your ego feel good now because you want to tear me down so badly!" she spat.

Morris looked puzzled. "Mia, what are you talking about? I never sent anything to your job. Why would I do something like that? Your job has nothing to do with us."

"So, you're going to lie to my face?" she quizzed.

"I wouldn't lie to you about something like that. It wasn't me," he said.

Mia relaxed her carriage and took deep breaths. If it wasn't him, then who, and then it hit her. Fucking Laurie! She covered her mouth at her realization. "Oh my God, Morris. I'm sorry for barging in like this. I'm so sorry."

"Mia, it's okay. I just don't understand why you'd think I would sabotage your job."

"I know, and I was wrong. It had to be Laurie," Mia said and then looked at Morris' colleagues who were gawking at her like she was a got'damn circus clown. "Listen, I'm sorry," she said and ran up out of his office.

"Mia, Mia, wait!" she heard him call out for her, but she kept on running. She was so embarrassed and felt so foolish. Why hadn't she even considered Laurie? She had blocked Rene completely, and after she called the boys in blue on his ass the night he showed up after Laurie threw his ass out, he hadn't shown up to her place again, so she had no idea what was going on with him or Laurie. She didn't know if he had also been on the chopping block at work. Mia got into her car and sped off fast. She saw Morris in her rearview and wondered why he even bothered coming after her. Saying sorry to him for the millionth time would have probably made him even more angry, so she was happy she got away from him before he caught up to her.

When she got home, she showered and cleaned her face. She was back in yoga pants, a sweat shirt and her hair was back into a sloppy bun. She wished her roommate hadn't moved out because she felt lonelier than ever, and she couldn't wait for NeNe and Legacy to arrive.

Chapter Thirty-Six

Reynard

"Is it straight?" Rey asked.

"It looks straight to me, baby. How about I hold it and then you see what you think," she said, and they exchanged places.

"Yes, it looks good right there. Mark it for me, babe," Rey said and handed her the pencil. She placed a little dot on the spot and handed him the picture. He then helped her off the step ladder. After Rey hung the last picture on the wall, they stood back and admired it.

"Your place turned out perfect, and this is so you."

"Thanks, babe," he said and pulled her close to give her a kiss. "I couldn't have done any of this without you, so thank you for everything. I would have never been able to coordinate any of this without you. You did a great job."

"You're welcome," she said.

"So, do you want to order take-out, go out or cook?" She crinkled her nose and then looked at the time. "It's a little late to cook don't you think? We could order pizza. I'm cool with a pizza."

"That'll work for me too." Rey pulled out his cell to check the closest pizza joints near his new place and ordered them a large, thin crust sausage pizza. She opened one of the bottles of wine she had brought over for them and poured them both a glass. They relaxed on the sofa and talked nonstop, listening to the smooth sounds of 90s

R&B. They sat close and flirted and couldn't keep their hands to themselves.

When the bell rang, Rey sprung to the door to get the pizza and then rushed right back to her side. They decided to eat in the living room, so Rey got up and grabbed a couple of paper plates, napkins and then refilled their glasses.

"So, can I ask you something?" she asked.

"Sure, you can ask me anything."

"Be careful, because people say that but then when they hear the question they freak out."

"True, but I promise I won't freak out," Rey said.

"Why did you and Anika break-up?"

"Oh wow," Rey smiled a sheepish grin. "You had to go there, huh?"

"Yes, because there were rumors circulating around the office and since I've never overheard Anika say it, I can't confirm it. The walls at work are paper thin, and other agents have heard some things."

"Okay, Camille, just be direct. What do you want to know?"

"Are you bi?" she quizzed.

"Hell no!" Rey said.

"Well, that means you're gay?"

"What the fuck kinda question is that, Camille?" She had rubbed Reynard the wrong way. He was feeling her and enjoying dating her, but he was tired of bitches asking him that silly ass question. Now that Lisa had returned to worked and working out, she didn't deny the rumors that he and Rey had hooked up before his surgery.

"Woe, calm down, Reynard. You said I could ask, so I'm asking. Why are you so defensive?"

"Because I get tired of people thinking I'm gay. I don't like men. I don't want to be with men, end of story."

"So, the one you cheated on Anika with wasn't a man, right?"

Rey leaned forward and put his drink on the table. He had to figure out a way to explain that he was attracted to Lisa, not his man parts. He had dabbled and did some things with Lisa that he still regretted, but he knew he never wanted to touch another dick other than his own ever in his life.

"Okay, Camille, I will be honest with you." He took a drink and then let out a deep breath. "Lisa was a transvestite man. He had his boob's done, hip injections, ass injections the whole nine. He had Lasik, so his face was smooth, and he was gorgeous when I first laid eyes on him. I thought he had some strong features, yes, but he looked like a real woman and even his voice was light. He'd have moments, after I'd gotten closer to him, where he'd act too flamboyant and I'd reel him in, but he was a woman in my eyes, except for his tool. He had planned to do the full surgery, which he did right before we broke up, but I'll admit I had sex with him more than a few times before the surgery. What's crazy is after the surgery, I never got to experience sex with his/her new body because it ended."

"It sounds like you really cared for him."

"I cared for him the person, and it's like I just never saw him as a man, if that makes sense. Like, if I was walking down the street and saw a dude looking like a dude, no fucking way would I get with him and if a gay dude tried, I might punch him in the motherfucking throat. I'm not bi or gay, and I love women, and if I ever run into a transgender person again and they don't have a pussy, I can't do it because my experiences with Lisa gives me regrets. I loved Lisa, I did, and now as a woman I think we could have had a great relationship, but if he hadn't gone through with the surgery, I know I would have ended it or cheated because I love women. And if this changes things with us, I understand, but I will not lie to another woman.

"I feel so shitty for what I did to NeNe, man, you just don't know. That woman was so good to me. She held me down even when I fucked up, and she deserved better than me. I'm glad she has it, and I hope that cat treats her right," Rey said.

"Thank you for being honest and it changes nothing, Rey. I like you, and I appreciate you for telling me about everything with Lisa. I'm not judging anyone."

"Since you are so liberal and understanding, what about you?"

"I was born a man," she joked, deepening her voice.

"You betta quit playing with me, Camille."

"Baby, I'm joking okay, it was a joke."

"I'm going to make you take off your clothes and prove it," he said.

"If that's what you want," she smiled.

He looked at her. His dick swelled at the thought of seeing her naked. "Answer the question first because you're just a little too calm about what I shared with you."

"Why, because I'm not ranting and raving and judging?"

"Exactly," he said.

"Listen, I am not gay or bi, I just know that you can't control a person's every move or thought process. I just want you faithful to me when you are with me. If we don't make it, hell, you can get with whoever you want to get with, but if you are with me just don't fuck with another man *or* woman. Simple! I'd rather my man be bi and faithful than be heterosexual and a whore. Cheating is cheating. It's like telling my man to not be attracted to other women. You can be attracted to whoever you like, but as long as you are with me, be with me. I don't care to share."

"Wow, that makes a lot of sense, Camille. I knew you were more than just a pretty face," Rey teased and pinched her nose. "So, what about that part about seeing you naked?" Rey said and ran his finger down the center of her breasts.

"Well, Rey, I will let you do anything you like as long as you have condoms."

"That's too easy," he said and kissed her deeply. They undressed and even though his leather sofa was brand new, he allowed her to straddle him. When she eased down on to him, Rey's dick throbbed because it felt so good to be inside of some pussy again. After and before Lisa's surgery, the last pussy he had felt was NeNe's, and Rey didn't want to erupt too soon, but she was winding and rolling on his dick so nice and smoothly, he knew he'd explode too fast. "Hold on, baby, your pussy got me ready, and I don't wanna bust yet," he groaned.

"Go ahead, baby, get that first one off for me," she moaned into his ear and then rolled her body harder, and Rey's mouth hung open because her pussy was so good. She was wet enough and damn sure tight enough, and Rey just let go. He didn't try to hold it back. She was right, he had to let that first one go, and he did.

"Ahhh, ahhh, ahhhhhh," he growled and tightened the grip he had on her ample cheeks. The cherry on top was her soft titties rubbing against his skin, and he grabbed hold of one and covered her solid nipple with his mouth until he had released all he had to give in that round. Her body felt like heaven. He lifted her off his rod, and her titties dangled in his face. Her skin was so soft, and he had forgotten how real tits and ass felt against his skin.

He had moments when he missed being with Lisa and missed his company, but since he connected with Camille, he thought of Lisa less and less. Now that he had gotten her goodies, he was for sure interested in something good with Camille, and if he had the chance to fall in love again, he'd never treat her the way he did NeNe. He had no more time for bullshit and games.

"Come on, baby, let me go flush this," he said. She moved to the side and fell back onto the couch.

"Hurry," she giggled.

"I'll be right back," he said and went to the bathroom that was off the kitchen on that floor. He opened the cabinet over the toilet and grabbed a wash cloth and ran hot water over it. He wiped down his dick and laid the towel on the vanity. By their relationship being so brand new, he grabbed another wash cloth, ran hot water over it and then took it to her.

"You can do it," she suggested. He didn't hesitate. He laid the hot towel over her center and did a nice wipe down. He took the towel back, tossed it in the sink and when he came back, she had one leg propped up on the back of the sofa and the other draped over the side rubbing her clit.

"Now that is some sexy shit right there, let me help you out," Rey offered. He went over to the sofa, got on the floor on his knees, wrapped his arms around her thick thighs and then pulled her pussy to his face. Her scent was right, so Rey dove in and devoured her nectar. Her sweet moans drove him over the edge, and his dick was hard enough to break bricks. He wanted her to cum so he could get back inside of her, so he pushed back her hood, giving him more access to her swollen bulb and put just the right amount of suction on it and pushed two fingers inside. Within seconds, she exploded, and her juices coated his fingers. He kissed her clit softly and rose to his feet. He smeared her juices from his fingers onto his erection and got another condom.

Camille rolled over and got on her knees, but Rey wanted her on her back. Every time he was with Lisa, he could never be on his back. Even though Rey could have penetrated him in the ass that way, he just never wanted to look down at his dick. Now that he could look down at a wet shiny pussy, he wanted her on her back with her legs spread as wide as she could spread them. He gave her a gentle tap on her ass.

"No, baby, I want you on your back please, and I want you to open wide for me. I want to see my dick sliding in and out of you," he panted because he was excited and ready. She did as ordered, and the sofa was the right height for him to go back down on his knees. He pulled her bottom as close to the edge as he could get her and then pushed her legs back so far, her elbows were behind her knees.

He looked down at it, and it was beautiful. Her hairs were nicely trimmed, only a little down the center, and the way it shined made his dick jump, and he got ready to slide in. He slapped her opening a few times and then grabbed hold of her thighs and let his head guide him on in.

"Whew," she breathed out. "Rey, ahhh, that feels good," she released.

"Yes, baby. Yo' pussy is so good, damn, shit!" he groaned. Rey kept his stroke easy and steady because he wanted to enjoy the feeling of her body, and it was damn good. After a while of stroking it steadily, he sped up and pumped harder. He rocked his hips side to side and slapped the back of her thighs as he rode her pussy hard and deep. He made sure he massaged her breasts and tweaked her nipples and went in for a kiss in between strokes. Her body was driving him crazy, and he could do her all night if she let him.

She called out his name, he called out hers. That shit was so good, Rey didn't want to cum without her getting another too, so he licked his fingers and rubbed her clit and continued to bang her tunnel. When he felt her walls contract, her breathing change and her moans grow louder, he let himself have one too.

After they cleaned up, Rey got the leather cleaner and wiped down the sofa. He then went upstairs and got a blanket and threw it over the leather. "I can't believe we did it on my brand new sofa bucket fucking naked."

"I know, babe, but that shit was good as hell," she smiled, nodding her head up and down.

"I ain't gon' lie, it was," he said and got up. "You want more wine?"

"Nah, I should get going."

"Get going? Why?"

"Because it's getting late, and I have work in the morning."

"Why can't you go to work from here?"

"Because I don't have any work clothes, and my make-up and stuff is at my place."

"Understood, but tomorrow, lunch right?"

"As long as you're paying," she teased.

"Is it my turn already?"

She grabbed her phone. "Let me check my calendar. Let's see, the last time it was me, but since you got dinner, lunch is on me tomorrow."

"Where have you been all my life?" he joked.

He kissed her goodnight at her car and then opened her door. She got in, and he stole one more kiss before she pulled away.

The next afternoon, he walked her into her office after their lunch date and ran into NeNe.

"Hey," he said.

"Hey, you're back again. I thought you closed on your house what, a couple of weeks ago?"

"About that or a little more."

"So you're here because," she dragged out the word because.

"Oh, I just dropped Camille off and came in to get her dry cleaning ticket. I'm going to grab it for her since she has a late showing."

"Oh, so the rumors are true, you and Camille are an item now. What happened to ole dude, umm, umm," she said snapping her finger in the air, like she was trying to recall.

"Lisa and I broke up a couple months ago."

"So, did you tell Camille that you're gay?"

"I told Camille everything, not like it's your business."

"Oh, well great."

"Thanks."

"Hey listen, Camille and I are not close, but she is one of the good ones, so don't screw her over, Rey. Her last relationship didn't end well and finally after almost two years, she's dating you, so act the fuck right," she advised.

"NeNe, I am not going to act up."

"Please don't. I remember the times when you were good, so be that guy, not the guy I broke up with," she admonished.

"I plan to be. How are you and Action Jaxson?"

NeNe burst out in laughter. "What did you say?"

"You heard me. I remember back in the day when you, Mia and Legacy used to sit in the living with your little girl talk and wine, and y'all would call him that."

"No, Mia calls him that," she continued to laugh. "And we are doing good."

"That's cool, NeNe. Well, it was nice catching up but I gotta get back to the gym."

"Sure, and good luck with Camille."

"Thanks," he said and walked away. It was strange that they were cordial, but when you're finally happy with your life, you don't harbor grudges or wish evil on the ones who did you dirty. *Forgiveness is a beautiful thing*, Rey thought as he headed back to work.

Chapter Thirty-Seven

Mia

"Girl, you should have been there to witness it. Tanya was shaking and shivering and shit acting like she was gon' pass out and trying to fall to the floor, but Kenny had a hold of that ass and would not let that ho hit the flo' you hear me," Legacy laughed as she shared the fake belly story. Mia hadn't laughed all day since she had gotten the news of being fired, so she welcomed the laughter.

"It's on the internet, girl. I know it is, because folks had they phone out, so it will surface soon," Legacy said. They talked about Tanya's crazy ass for a little while longer, and then NeNe filled them in on Michelle, or as NeNe called her, *Katie Ka-Boom*.

"Lay, this bitch came at me in the bathroom at her momma's repast. What crazy ho' does that shit? She should be grieving the loss of her mother, not trying to scare off her soon to be ex-husband's new fiancé."

"Desperate ho's don't give a shit. You see Tanya walked around with a ten-pound silicone fake ass belly for months trying to get Kenny back. I hope she gets some help because that's just some crazy shit."

"Girl, the stress I'd be under knowing that there will be no baby by my supposed due date. I'd be a basket case," Mia said.

"Just count yo' blessings, Lay, because as sad as it was that she miscarried, Kenny don't have no kids out there with another woman."

"True that. If Morris and I would have stayed together, he may have had a child with Victoria."

"Speaking of Victoria. Mia, I got something to tell you after NeNe finishes telling us what happened in the bathroom with Katie Ka-Boom."

"It's not too much more to tell. I mean, she was meaning mugging and foaming at the mouth talking about how dirty she can play, and I told that bitch she wasn't the only one who can play dirty. I got up in her face, nose damn near touching, and told that bitch I'd slay her ass, and she stood there like a lil bitch. She didn't want none of this," NeNe said with hand gestures. Mia and Legacy were rolling.

"What if that bitch would have hit yo' ass?" Legacy asked between laughs.

"Chile, I would've got my ass beat because that was the Grey Goose talking,'" NeNe giggled.

"Oh shit, I wish I could have been there," Mia said, still laughing.

"Well, that shit worked. That ho was at the door apologizing to Jaxson like she was in a damn confession booth," NeNe joked. The girls were so tickled, they continued to joke and make fun of Tanya and Michelle until Legacy changed the subject.

"So, Mia, I must tell you about Victoria, Morris' ex-wife."

"Bitch, how you just know everybody?" NeNe said. "You knew Lisa, and now you know Victoria."

"I know right. Well, that dude I told y'all about, Omari, right."

"Omari, Omari, oh shit bitch, I already know where you're going. Morris has said that motherfucker's name a thousand times. How on earth, Legacy?"

"Mia, I don't fucking know. Anyway, she was in my chair when you came in Saturday."

"No way, no fucking way. That was the pregnant chick that was getting ready for her baby shower?"

"Yes!"

"Why the hell didn't you say something to me Saturday? I came in there looking all busted, and you didn't warn me?"

"Mia, I didn't figure that shit out until after you left. Well, after she helped me figure it out."

"How she know me?"

"Come on, Mia. Your name had to come up in some conversation, and you were at court that day with him, remember?"

"Yes, and she sho' wasn't that pregnant. Either I was too upset to recognize her or that baby weight gon' be a son of a bitch to lose," Mia joked.

"Yo' skinny ass always gotta crack on somebody's weight," NeNe said.

"NeNe, you didn't see her though," Mia said.

"Bitch, shut yo' skinny ass up before I force feed your ass a bacon sandwich," Legacy joked.

Mia shot her a look. "Anyway, did she have the baby yet?"

"Yep, as a matter of fact, she went into labor that night and had the baby the next morning."

"Damn, Morris must be on edge. All he used to say is for the baby's sake he hoped it's his, but he just didn't want Victoria as his kid's mother."

"Same shit Kenny used to say about Tanya, but don't worry, Morris is in the clear. That baby looks just like Omari."

"When did you see the baby?"

"Yesterday. I went by her place to see him, and that is Omari's seed fo' sho."

"Wow, I wonder if Morris knows?"

"Victoria says he saw the baby and still wanted the test, so I guess he wants to be one-hundred percent sure."

"I guess, but you know we have to ask about these pictures?" Legacy said.

"What's to ask? Y'all saw them, and that bitch Laurie sent them to my boss."

"That bitch wasn't playing when she said she was done with Rene, huh?"

"I don't know. She could be back with him. They could be separated. I don't know, and I don't give a fuck. I just want Rene to stay away from me."

"Mia, how you going to be so pissed at Rene when you went back to him for sex?" NeNe asked.

"Because I am! He was like my fucking kryptonite, and I hate him for that reason. I hate him for lying to me about him and Laurie's situation in the beginning. I hate him for lying to me telling me he was going to leave her. I hate that he sat there holding her hand and looking at me like I was the whore. I just hate him, NeNe, fuck!" she yelled.

"Mia, I hear all the shit you're saying, but you played the same game Rene played."

Her eyes welled. "I know, Lay, okay," she said and swiped a tear from her face. "I know I was wrong, but it's like if I blame him, I can live with myself."

"Well, you have to stop blaming him and forgive yourself for what you've done," NeNe advised. "We can sit here and blame them all day. I can blame Rey for fucking around with that dude all that time, but I allowed him to do me that way. He was wrong, yes, but I blame myself for staying."

Mia was quiet for a few moments, and they all sat in silence. "You're right, NeNe. We all played a part in the shit we've been through. I just wish I could have been wiser. I miss Morris so fucking much, and it's like my mind is in overload with how to get him back, but I'll never get him back," she said and just let the tears roll.

"Mia, here. Drink up," Legacy said, handing her her glass from the coffee table. "You will be all right, my friend. It will just take some time. You will meet someone else."

"But he won't be like Morris," she whined.

"How do you know that, he could be better," NeNe said. They all laughed.

Mia wiped her face one more good time and said, "Well, I won't be sitting around here moping about Morris for long."

"Oh, now you're good?" Legacy teased.

"No, bitch," Mia said and tossed a throw pillow at Legacy. "I have to look for another job."

"That's true," NeNe agreed.

Ding-Dong

Mia's doorbell rang. They all looked at each other.

"Are you expecting someone?" Legacy asked.

Mia put her glass down and stood. "No," she answered and went for the door. She went on her toes and looked through the peephole. "Oh shit, it's Morris," she whispered, holding her chest.

"Morris?"

"Yes, bitch, Morris," NeNe said to Legacy.

"What do I do?"

"You can start by opening the door, crazy," NeNe said.

"Look at me," Mia said, pointing to her clothes.

Ding Dong

"Mia, open the damn door," Legacy said.

Mia turned to the door and undid the locks and opened it.

"Hey, Mia. Can we talk?" Morris asked.

"Sure, come on in," Mia said and let him in. "These are my friends, Legacy and NeNe," she introduced.

"Hello, ladies. It's nice to finally put a face with a name. I heard more than a little about you two."

"And we heard a boat load of shit about you too," Legacy snapped.

Mia shot her a look. "Morris, what brings you by? I mean, this is super unexpected."

NeNe stood. "Well, Legacy and I will get out of here to give you two some privacy," NeNe said, taking her coat from the back of the chair.

"You can go, I ain't ready to go," Legacy said.

"Girl, if you don't get yo' high yellow ass up out that chair," NeNe spat.

"What you gon' do, slay me?" Legacy joked, making them all laugh.

"You two are too much," Mia chuckled. They both went to kiss and hug Mia goodbye and once Mia closed the door, she turned her attention back to Morris. "Can I take your coat?"

"Yes, thank you." He took it off and handed it to her. She went over to the coat rack by the door and hung it up.

"Have a seat," Mia offered.

"Thank you." He sat down.

Mia sat in the chair where Legacy had been sitting and waited on him to speak, but he just stared at her. "I know I look a mess, Morris, but considering the day I had, I believe I'm entitled."

"You still look beautiful to me," he said.

She looked away and then back at him. "So, what did you want to talk about?"

"Us, but somehow I don't know where to begin. I drove here rehearsing what I'd say, but now that I'm here it's like I can't remember my lines."

"Well, speak from your heart and forget about what you rehearsed," Mia suggested, and tried to fight the urge to cry, but that was useless. She loved this man and hated where they were at the moment. She just sat there and swiped each tear while waiting on him to speak.

"I'm not good at forgiving people, and I'm certainly not a guy of second chances, so I took your cheating on me as an unjustifiable offense. I could not understand how you could love me and betray me in such a way. Because of me being such a martinet who refused to accept your apology, I didn't allow myself to forgive you, so how could I say that I love you and not want to give you a do-over? I may not have made the same mistakes that you have, but I've made them. I may not have hurt a person the way you have hurt me, but I have hurt people, and I hurt someone I loved.

"When I was with Victoria, I was a workaholic. My motto was work hard now and lay back later, but I married a woman who was ready to be with her husband and not at home alone. I married a woman who wasn't power hungry or a go get'em like me, and my mistake was marrying her before I got my feet off the ground. Victoria didn't deserve all those lonely nights, or the times I'd get so busy I'd forget we had plans, or I'd come home and my dinner would be so damn cold in the microwave because I was hours, not minutes, late. I threw gifts at Victoria. I let her shop till she dropped, but that didn't give her what she needed. The point is, I loved her, Mia, I truly did, but love wasn't enough to make me slow down. Love wasn't enough to make me cut my business trips short, and love wasn't enough to make me impregnate my wife.

"Victoria told me she was lonely, more than once, more than twice and she didn't lie to me about how she was feeling. She begged me to give her a baby at least, so she could have something—a part of me while I was away, but I was so focused on what I wanted and what I desired that I didn't give her what she wanted or what she desired. I know you love me, Mia, but it wasn't enough to keep you committed to me, and I forgive you. I miss you and would like a second chance with you."

"Wait a minute. You're asking *me* for a second chance?"

"Yes."

"But I fucked up."

"You did, and when you asked me for a second chance my answer was no, so now I'm asking you," he said, looking her in her eyes.

"Can I have some time to think about it?" His eyes widened. "Baby, I'm playing," she said and stood. She walked over and stood in front of him. "Of course you can have a second chance, Morris. I'd give you a thousand chances. I love you, and I am sorry I hurt you and I swear on everything that Rene is history and I'd never treat you that way ever again. What you have is enough for me. I didn't get it before, but now I do and all I want is you Morris."

"I know, and I love you too," he said and kissed her. He pulled her onto his lap, and they sat back on the sofa. "Oh, and another thing."

"What is it?"

"I know Victoria's baby isn't mine."

"Did you get the results back already?"

"I don't need them, that boy looks just like Omari."

"Oh, wow."

"Yep, so I guess things just turned out how they were supposed to for all of us."

"If you say so," she sighed. "I'm out of a job, remember?"

"And you're stressed because?"

"I gotta find a new job, duh," she laughed.

"Mia, I own my own company."

"And?"

"I can give you a job, duh," he joked.

"Oh my God, baby, for real? I don't have to go on unemployment."

"Not unless you want to."

"Oh, hell no. So, let's talk salary."

"As long as we can discuss it naked."

"Sounds good to me, baby," Mia purred and kissed him.

Morris was right. Things turned out how they were supposed to for all of them because they all went on to live happy and healthy lives. Sometimes feelings can get you in or out of trouble. Being in your feelings for someone only counts if they are in their feelings for you. If they're not, be in your damn feelings for yourself and move the hell on!

The End!!!

Note from the Author

Readers thank you for your support, and I truly hope you enjoy this story about love, relationships and lies. I know there were some head shaking moments and some mouth dropping actions in this story that made you scratch your head. Remember, its fiction for some but could be a reality for others. Thank you again for being an Anna Black fan and know that I not only do this for me, I do this to entertain you. Your feedback is super important to me, so I can know your thoughts about my desire to deliver good, fun-filled and entertaining stories.

I hope you guys enjoyed part 2 of "Sometimes I'm In my Feelings." Please spread the word, leave a review and check out my other novels, short stories and novella's. You can find me on FACEBOOK, TWITTER and INSTAGRAM, and you can also email me at bookannablack@gmail.com.

Be You, Do You, Love You

Happy Reading!!!

CPSIA information can be obtained
at www.ICGtesting.com
Printed in the USA
LVOW05s0411290817
546756LV00005B/21/P